THE BEST PRANK BOOK EVER!

By Tarrin P. Lupo

Porcupine Publications

Porcupine Publications

ISBN 978-1-937311-05-6

Printed with the spirit of

I dedicate this to my dog Schroeder who truly understood the art of a good practical joke!

Disclaimer

In my younger years, I did a lot of acts that I would never do now. I am sharing these because they are funny. Use some basic common sense and do not do anything that will damage property or hurt someone. Don't do any of these that can get you arrested! If you do use any of these pranks, use them on people that will appreciate a good joke. Otherwise, it could blow up in your face.

Table of Contents

.

Introduction

Sometimes revenge ideas are just what the doctor ordered to get even. In some cases a prescription for safe office pranks are perfect for some fun lighthearted payback. Other times getting serious revenge may be necessary, like getting even with ex-girlfriends or ex-boyfriends. This book's revenge ideas run the full gamut of pranks. You can find a safe practical joke to play on your coworkers, family members or boss. You can also find a way to utterly ruin the life of your lying, cheating spouse.

Most children loved Christmas but my favorite holiday was always April Fool's Day. For as long as I can remember, I loved pulling tricks on my friends and family. Later in life things changed and people became much more difficult to deal with. I had run-ins with scam artists, cheating girlfriends, difficult and annoying neighbors and so on. I realized I needed to find a nastier way to deal with these jerks. These people deserved a more intense form of payback. I began studying the fine art of revenge and getting even. I became a master at it over the years.

I now wish to share what has taken me years to compile. Some of these tales are very funny and some are very cruel. Most ideas and pranks have been around forever and are considered classics. In this book you may find plenty of classics that you might have done as a kid but are still damn funny.

I have tried to add a new twist to give these old classics new life. I am proud to offer you four times the amount of pranks per idea – the original idea and three prank upgrades. Here you will be able to find a trick that is just right for your situation.

We love funny stories, new ideas and pictures of pranks. So please contact me on my site http://TheBestPrankBookEver.LupoLit.com/. If I use it I will be happy post it with your name and give you kudos.

I hope you enjoy the more than 100 revenge ideas and hope you find the perfect tool to get even!

Good Hunting,

Tarrin P. Lupo

Nemesis - Greek spirit of divine retribution - comes from a Greek word meaning "to give what is due".

Chapter 1
OFFICE PRANK IDEAS

There are so many fun ways to screw with your office workers for your own entertainment. The 9 to 5 rat race is depressing enough, so the only way to keep your job fun is to stir up some mischief. Do you have an annoying boss or coworker who is just begging for a prank to be pulled on them? Well then, let me help with some revenge ideas. A word of warning here, some of these tricks can possibly make your boss or coworkers very mad. Unless your boss or coworkers have a great sense of humor I would stay under the radar and strike anonymously. Even though you want to make your office life much more interesting I don't think it would be too funny to get fired. Be careful with who you pull these on, because some people cannot take a joke.

WATER COOLER PRANKS

You will need a water cooler in your office to have fun with this next set of pranks. These gags are pretty safe pranks to pull and shouldn't get you fired. The first revenge idea is to simply add salt to the water cooler. Sure you will ruin a whole jug of water but it will be worth it for some fun.

Prank Idea Upgrades

EVIL PRANK BONUS

Another version of this prank is to salt the cups. If the cooler has a sleeve of cups pull them all out. Load the bottom of the cups with salt and put the sleeve back in place. Most victims won't even check their cup before filling it up. Sit in the break room and watch the parade of victims spit salt water everywhere.

GETTING EVEN BONUS

If the sleeve of cups are cone shaped, poke very tiny holes in the bottom of them. When the victim fills up the cup it will soak them. Another prank you can use is to switch the hot and cold water buttons. These should pop right off most old coolers. If the buttons don't come off just paint the buttons blue and red. If your cooler gets really hot you might not want to do this and burn some someone's mouth, unless they deserve it.

GETTING SERIOUS REVENGE BONUS

Sick of your office manager? Make them spend a bunch of their time dealing with a constantly leaking water cooler. Take a thick needle and poke a bunch of holes in the bottom of the jug. The holes shouldn't be noticed because the plastic is very thick at the bottom, this will mess up the pressure in the jug. Now the fun begins! The water will slowly start to flow out of the jug and drip onto the floor. The water will leak slowly so most people probably won't notice for a few hours. Ideally, you should do this before a weekend so the water really gets a chance to flow.

If you make the holes small enough that they weren't noticed by the office manager, they may think that the dispenser is broken, and the office will pay to have it fixed. Wait a week and strike again. As an added bonus, they might think the dispenser is broken and throw the whole unit out. Take it out of the trash and take it home to enjoy or sell it.

FAX AND COPIER PRANKS

Although fax machine technology is on its way out, many offices still have them. It is fun to screw with copiers, too. Let's start with the pranks for fax machines. The oldest fax machine prank is to simply send your victim a solid black sheet about 50 times. When the victim's fax starts printing, it will completely burn up their ink. This used to actually break old fax machines that could not handle that much printing. This might not break a fax machine, but since ink cost so much now it will really make them mad.

Prank Idea Upgrades

EVIL PRANK BONUS

The never-ending fax is another classic that still is funny. Write a funny message or get a funny picture of the victim and print it out. Make 3-4 copies of the print out and glue them end to end. Make sure all the pages are facing the same direction. Call your victims fax number and load in the long sheet. Wait for 2 pages to be sent and then quickly glue the first page to the last page so it creates an endless loop. The message will continually be sent over and over until somebody cuts the paper.

GETTING EVEN BONUS

The copy machine is fun to mess with too. Of course, the classic prank is to copy your butt. A word of caution, if you weigh too much you will fall through the glass and hurt yourself. Another fun prank is to use a dry erase marker or a permanent one if you know you are getting fired shortly. Write a funny message like "Lance likes your grandmother!" on the glass of the copier. Most people don't even look at the glass before they use the copier. If you are really lucky they will copy a whole stack of papers by using the document feeder treys. They will probably walk off while the copier goes to work and will be pretty mad when their entire stack of copies has your message all over it.

GETTING SERIOUS REVENGE BONUS

If you want to be even stealthier you can add just a few selective sheets of a funny message into the copier's stack of blank supply papers. This way when people copy a whole stack of stuff, just a few gag sheets will be hidden in the stack. They probably will be discovered much later and it will be impossible to pin it on you. If you get really lucky your company will fax those copies out without seeing the messages and they will spread to another office like a virus!

PHONE PRANKS

Screwing with a coworker's phone can be great fun. Office phones are the last bastion of land line phones. Unfortunately, cell phones have ruined these pranks in the private world. Here are some safe pranks that should not get you fired. A classic prank is to wrap the phone in tin foil or plastic wrap. Another safe prank is to screw with co-worker's phone buttons. Take off the buttons that transfer calls and switch them around. Whenever the victim transfers a call it will be directed to the wrong extension or the caller will be disconnected.

Prank Idea Upgrades

EVIL PRANK BONUS

You can glue the receiver to the base so it rings and rings and they can't pick it up. Or just steal the receiver cord so when the phone rings they will pick up a receiver but there will not be any sound.

GETTING EVEN BONUS

You can use the receiver to attack your victim. If you want to be sneaky put self tanner on the ear piece. Every time they pick up the phone their ear will get a little darker. If you want real fun and their phone is black, use shoe polish. This will be hard to get off their hair and ear.

GETTING SERIOUS REVENGE BONUS

The best office phone prank should be used on new employees. The first day when a new person is hired volunteer to show them how the phone works. Tell the new employee they must hit the intercom button in order to dial out of the office. The new employee will probably call out sometime that day. If you are lucky everyone in the office will get to share his personal phone calls. If you can get everyone in the office in on this prank it can be extremely funny.

If you don't like someone in your office and you want to get them in trouble with their spouse or current partner use this next prank. When the spouse or partner calls looking for them, say sorry he/she is on the phone with their girlfriend/boyfriend right now, can I take a message? When the spouse gets upset and says, "Get him on the phone. This is his wife!" Just say, "Oh, oops!" and hang up on them.

MOUSE PRANKS

These are fun pranks to do to people who are not real computer savvy. You would be amazed at how technologically dysfunctional some people can be. You would be stunned at how dumbfounding this first prank can be to someone. Simply pull the mouse cord out a little so the mouse no longer works. I did this to an employee that worked for me and she seriously was stumped for almost 10 minutes. She had no idea how to interface with a computer without a mouse.

Prank Idea Upgrades

EVIL PRANK BONUS

Torturing this employee became my new entertainment. She finally got smart enough to check the cord so I had to use a new idea. I decided to attack the track ball in the mouse. I replaced it with a gum ball that I licked and chewed a little on one side. The mouse barely worked and then became very sticky and made a huge mess. She figured this one out pretty quickly so I put the original track ball back. Since the mouse was almost ruined from the gum I decided to just glue the ball down, she was not amused.

GETTING EVEN BONUS

The gum ball and glue destroyed the mouse so I purchased a new optical one for the office. I left her alone for a day or two and then I put a piece of tape over the optical light. It took her a very long time to figure this one out.

GETTING SERIOUS REVENGE BONUS

The final thing I did was to go into the mouse settings and change them. I reversed her mouse directions, made it super sensitive and changed the buttons around. Since she understood nothing about computers she just gave up and moved to a different computer.

Ghost Computer Prank

I also used this prank on my employees. Why anyone would work for me I have no idea. This works best if your employee who has very little computer knowledge. The easiest thing is to just change the victim's screen saver or wallpaper. I put up a very unflattering picture in which a female employee thought she looked extremely fat. You can imagine how mad she was when that picture was the wallpaper on all the office computers and she had no idea how to change it.

Prank Idea Upgrades

EVIL PRANK BONUS

I decided to continue torturing this employee by messing with her screen saver. You can make a dirty screen saver or I would make it say mean things about her fellow employees. So the office would go to lunch and the screen saver would kick on and say something insulting. The message would be like "Jennifer really thinks her new haircut looks good, Ha Ha ..... Meg". Jennifer got pissed off at Meg but it was great fun.

GETTING EVEN BONUS

I then decided to convince her that her computer was haunted. In order for you to pull this off you have to get the computers close enough to each other. Side-by-side cubicles work the best for this prank. Get the computers close enough to switch the monitor cords. Jennifer would sit down and I could see her move the mouse on my screen. I sent a message to her screen saying, "STOP TOUCHING MY MOUSE!" Then I would write, "Touch my mouse slower and softer. Yeah, that's it, baby!" Use your imagination and have some fun with this one. By the way those are not really my employees' names. I changed their names to protect their identity.

GETTING SERIOUS REVENGE BONUS

The last thing you can do is spy on your coworkers. This can get you in MAJOR hot water, but what do you care? You will have enough blackmail information on all your coworkers and boss. Perhaps you will never get fired. Most employees are not technically savvy enough to understand networking. If all the office computers are on the same network you have accessibility everyone else's monitors. Actually if you're the boss and own the computers it is completely legal to do this to your employees. A much better solution is to install a key logger which will let you see everything a person does on their computer.

MEAN COWORKER PRANKS

Sometimes coworkers can be unbearable to deal with. Instead of openly dealing with your problems like an adult, I recommend childish, passive-aggressive pranks. Simply drive your coworker crazy until they quit or blow up at work and appear unstable. Here are some great ways to convince them to quit. The first thing to do make them unproductive as hell so they get way behind on their workload and the boss will get angry with them. The easiest way is to do this is to call them at least 30 times a day and hang up. This is especially funny if your victim has to say, "Hello, this is Pam. How can I help you?" 30 times a day. Make sure you call from a blocked line and stay out of site when you do this.

Prank Idea Upgrades

EVIL PRANK BONUS

Wait until the victim walks away and you can mess with their computer without being caught. Open their word processor program and set up auto correct to change legitimate words into misspelled words as they are typed. Then go to their password settings and change it to a bunch of random letters. The next morning when they get in and turn on the computer, they won't be able to get past the new password. They will waste most of the day waiting on some IT guy to show up and fix it. They will lose a whole day of work dealing with this and the boss will get pissed at their incompetence. Wait a few days and repeat. Make them look like they are stupid as hell and keep accidentally changing their password.

GETTING EVEN BONUS

Mess with the boss's food, and plant the empty bag in your victims trash can. When the boss gets mad about their missing lunch, play stupid. Eventually, the boss will start looking around and find the planted evidence. Nothing gets you fired faster than messing with the boss's stuff.

GETTING SERIOUS REVENGE BONUS

Step up the Mean Coworker Pranks by getting the victim fired. Hopefully you have done all three of the above pranks to get your boss pissed at your victim. Now start sending anonymous emails about how you worked with the victim at their previous place of employment. Warn the boss to keep a careful eye on them because they can't be trusted. Continue by saying they cost their last company a ton of money because they wasted so much time on the phone and kept screwing up the computers around the office. MAKE SURE YOU HIDE YOUR IP ADDRESS if you are going to do this, so the email doesn't come back and get you fired.

Send it from a public library or coffee shop if you can't hide your IP address. Hopefully the boss will keep a hawk eye on them and you just need to keep making the victim unproductive until they are fired.

GET A COWORKER FIRED

For those coworkers that are too annoying to deal with. It's best to annoy the hell out of them so they either quit or your boss cans them. Here are some fun revenge ideas to help that annoying coworker move on. Do things to annoy them: glue the wheels of their office chair. When they push a good push on their chair it will topple over. Who knows? Maybe they will get hurt and go on workers' comp.

Prank Idea Upgrades

EVIL PRANK BONUS

Send a memo that only the coworker will receive stating that everyone has tomorrow off because of the boss's religious beliefs. If you get lucky, the employee won't show up.

GETTING EVEN BONUS

If your office has a no smoking policy then you will want to take advantage of that. Get a bunch of used cigarettes and an ashtray and then hide it in your victim's work area. Eventually someone will find it if you keep complaining about smelling smoke in the office.

GETTING SERIOUS REVENGE BONUS

When your coworker goes to lunch, hack into their personal e-mail and send all their private mail to your boss and other coworkers. Make sure to include yourself in your list of coworkers to throw off the blame. The boss will be thrilled that the victim sends out all this personal stuff on company time. The easiest way is to go through their instant messaging (IM). A lot of people screw off at work and talk to their friends on IM. There is a good chance that when you click their IM logo it will immediately open the mail account associated with it. Don't forget to dig through their chat history and send those to. Make sure the chat history includes the time and date stamps so the boss knows they are chatting during work hours.

If you really want to see and capture all their passwords and see EVERYTHING they are doing then install a key logger on their computer.

CUBICLE PRANKS

Screwing with your coworker's cubicles help pass the time. These pranks are safe to pull and should not get you fired. Let's start with a basic cubicle prank. Just use plastic or paper to completely wrap the cubicle up.

If you want to take it one step further you can wet the paper down with glue and water. Take your time and make a huge papier-mâché desk. If you are talented enough you can cut the desk out and remove it. The victim will think their desk is just wrapped with paper. They will be shocked to find out it is only a paper shell.

Prank Idea Upgrades

EVIL PRANK BONUS

Build a cubicle robot out of office boxes. Have some fun and make a huge robot and/or an Easter Island one.

GETTING EVEN BONUS

Get a bunch of packing peanuts and fill the cubicle completely full. This will make a huge mess to clean up so try to remain anonymous. You will have to probably do this over a weekend when you can get the office to yourself for a while. If you want to be a big jerk put a bunch of the peanuts through the shredder first. Shredded peanuts are almost impossible to pick up because they cling to everything and get mashed into the carpet easily.

GETTING SERIOUS REVENGE BONUS

A fun cubicle prank is to lay little cups of water all over the cubicle floor. You can use your imagination and fill the cups with other fluids if you really don't like your coworker. You can fill them with copier ink and water or glue mixed with water. Either of those will be impossible to clean up or will stain the victims feet and ankles. If you use enough cups it will make it impossible to get to their desk without knocking some of the cups over and spilling a bunch of fluid.

More Cubicle Pranks

Work gets pretty dull so you need some good office pranks to help pass the time. These are some safe cubicle pranks. They should not get you fired, but a few of them might really cheese off your coworkers. One of the simplest pranks is using birthday balloons. Tie them to the ceiling using a bag or net. Tie a string to the bag or net of balloons so when you pull the strings the balloons fall down. When the victim steps into the cubicle, drop them down all over their head.

Prank Idea Upgrades

EVIL PRANK BONUS

You can unscrew the walls of the cubicle so when they are touched, they will fall in on the victim. Warning: this can injure your victim if the cubicle walls are heavy.

GETTING EVEN BONUS

If a coworker breaks their foot or leg you can do this office prank. This is especially funny if the victim has to use a wheelchair. Paint a handicap parking spot in the cubicle. You can also use tape to make a handicap parking sign.

Or if they are not suffering an injury and you still want to get even, then tape the outline of a body and surround their cubicle with crime scene tape.

GETTING SERIOUS REVENGE BONUS

One of the funniest pranks is to completely steal the cubicle. You will need some friends to help you do this quickly. Disassemble the cubicle and reassemble it in the parking lot or in the grass. Make sure you reassemble the cubicle just the way it was with all the pictures and desk supplies in the correct place.

If you have enough time and man power you can completely set up the whole office in the parking lot. Reassemble all the cubicles, trash cans and even the water cooler.

MORE COMPUTER PRANKS

For all of these pranks, you will need access to the victim's computer for a short time. This prank would be ideal for an office or roommate situation. These are safe, silly pranks that are just annoying to people. An easy prank to pull is to screw with the power options. This works on non-computer savvy victims. Here is how to do it: Go to start. Then, control panel. Then power options. You will want to select "turn off monitor to 1 min". This will cause the monitor to turn off every minute that it is not being used. This becomes incredibly annoying if the victim can't figure out why this is happening. Be a real jerk and also set the hard disks to turn off every three minutes.

Free Revenge Ideas Upgrades

EVIL PRANK BONUS

Another fun thing to do is to change someone's sounds. You can record your voice saying funny things and replace the normal sound accompanied computer functions. Have some fun and do your best Mr. T impression saying, "Welcome, fool!" or "Access denied, jive turkey fool!" Don't forget to turn the sound up. You will be able to set your own sounds by going to start, then control panel, and then accessibility options.

GETTING EVEN BONUS

Have some real fun and screw with the language option. Be sure to change their password first, and then change the language on the computer. Choose an Asian or Middle East dialect so they can't figure out how to even do basic functions. Here is how you change the language. Go to start, control panel, then regional and language options and finally pick a language.

GETTING SERIOUS REVENGE BONUS

This classic prank has been around for awhile but it is great, especially if the victim is not computer savvy. It will completely stump your victim. This prank makes their desktop look functional but nothing will work.

Here is how to do it. Take a screen shot of victim's desktop. Right click desktop, arrange icons, and then click show desktop icons. Click this so that icons are hidden.

Next, right click tool bar, then select properties and then take off lock the tool bar and put on auto-hide. Lastly, set desktop picture as desktop.

Now, when the victim tries to open anything on their page they will think something is wrong with their computer. The victim will try and open their folders and nothing will happen.

DESK PRANKS

Some of these ideas are pretty safe and shouldn't get you fired. Be aware that some people REALLY love their desk chotchkies or trinkets and it can really make them angry. Feel out your victim first. Here is a very safe prank idea that won't damage anything. Wrap your victim's desk in paper, plastic shipping wrap or tin foil. Make sure you wrap up every single item and then tape it up with packing tape so they take forever to open.

Prank Idea Upgrades

EVIL PRANK BONUS

The next step in this prank is to get extra strong glue and glue everything down. Be creative! Like when you glue the stapler down, glue it to the side of the desk. But only glue the bottom so the stapler still works.

GETTING EVEN BONUS

Have some real fun and piss the whole office off by gluing everybody's stuff to your victim's desk. Make sure to include a few of your own things to throw the blame off you.

GETTING SERIOUS REVENGE BONUS

This last office prank is famous and is even featured on a well-known television comedy. Even though it is famous, it is still worth doing because it causes a great laugh around the office. Steal an item off the victim's desk that they really like or work with everyday. Take it home and make a bowl of clear Jell-O. Suspend the object in the Jell-O by making the Jell-O first and then cutting it open and placing the object in the middle. After it freezes, bring it back to the office and return it to the desk.

Chapter 2
ROOMMATE REVENGE

Living with roommates, family and significant others can really wear you down.

The only defense you have to protect your own sanity is to take solace in pranking others you live with. Part of the fun of sharing a house with someone is the ability to pull gags on them. Some of the revenge ideas can get you in hot water, but trust me they are still worth doing. These pranks are light hearted and you might have even used some of them on your brothers and sisters. I have tried to put a twist on the old classics so check them all out. These pranks can definitely be turned up to the serious revenge level to run off an annoying roommate or to simply torture your family members for your own amusement. Most of these pranks you can do with everyday items, but sometime it is worth it to check out the professional prank stores.

TRASHCAN SOAKED REVENGE

I dusted off this old classic to because it is still fun to use. There are many variations of this one. The old school way is to use a small trash can placed on the top of a slightly opened door. You need to balance it just right so when the door swings open the trash can will turn over and spill on the victim. If you lined it up right the water and trashcan will fall on top of your victim's head.

Another version of this is to lean a trash can full of water against the door, or stack a bunch of cups full of water against the door. You want the door to swing inward if you want to lean a trashcan against the door. You want the door to swing outward if you stack a bunch of cups in front of the door.

Revenge Idea Upgrades

EVIL PRANK BONUS

Ice water is always more fun but it requires timing. Another nice variation is to pour ice water onto someone while they are taking a shower.

You can also throw water mixed with blue drink mix packs or food coloring while they're in the shower. I recommend drink mix packs over ink because ink can really burn someone's eyes. Try to avoid nailing them in the eyes when you throw the blue staining drink mix packs or food coloring on them.

GETTING EVEN BONUS

Include things that are impossible to clean up in the water. Things like fried beans, pepper and anything that is a small enough particle to get into the rug and be a real chore to get out.

GETTING SERIOUS REVENGE BONUS

Pee in the bucket or use old sewage water.

TRIPWIRE REVENGE

I was first introduced to trip wires and booby traps by my older brother who would use them on me for his amusement. I was a quick study and started learning how to lay my own more elaborate traps. Let's start with the basics, the simple tripwire. People rarely watch their feet when they walk and this is an invitation to attack such a vulnerable area. Here is how to set one up. All you need are two nails or large thumb tacks and some fishing wire. You want to place the nails or tacks about four inches off the ground on each side of the door frame. String the line very tightly and enjoy watching your victim fall on their face.

Revenge Idea Upgrades

EVIL PRANK BONUS

You can put shaving cream on the floor. Knock on the door and run, when the person opens it and walks out they will fall right into the shaving cream. Be sure you can run faster than your victim.

GETTING EVEN BONUS

Set your trip line and combine it with the Trashcan Soaked Revenge.

GETTING SERIOUS REVENGE BONUS

Use the trip wire to have your victim fall into mouse traps or tacks.

You can do a modern day tar-and-feathering. Set the tripwire up so they fall into a glue feather mix.

Another more authentic looking version of this is to have your victim fall into motor oil and glue and feathers. The motor oil will give it the tar look you want without having to use real tar. Try to use white down feathers because they seem to be very messy once oil gets into them.

I did once witness a hazing ritual where they tied the victim up and glued corn kernels all over him. They then blind folded him and set a bunch of chickens loose. Supposedly, their little beaks are kind of sharp because the victim did not enjoy getting pecked, although I thought it was hilarious to watch.

FLOOR TRAPS AND SCORPIONS

These are land mines for victims who walk around with bare feet. I was first introduced to this by one of my best friends. When we were kids my best friend used twisted paper clips or staples and made "scorpions" to keep his barefoot grandmother from snooping around his room.

These "scorpions" are cheap, easy to make and hurt like hell without really injuring someone. I prefer the staple method because they are smaller and fairly invisible. Basically you take two staples and twist them together in the middle so the ends stick out in every direction. Place these all over the floor for your barefooted-victim.

Revenge Idea Upgrades

EVIL PRANK BONUS

You can also put these in chairs. Most people don't look before they sit. These work best in wooden seats like school desk chairs or metal chairs.

If you can pull it off, you can also put them on toilet seats. To make this prank work you will probably have to unscrew the bathroom light bulb so the victim has to go to the bathroom in the dark.

GETTING EVEN BONUS

If you share a Jack and Jill bathroom or connected bathroom you can have even more fun. Wait until your victim falls asleep and sneak in. Put the "scorpions" on the floor around the toilet and enjoy. To make things more exciting unscrew the light bulbs, when your victim gets up for a midnight bathroom run - you will hear the yelling.

GETTING SERIOUS REVENGE BONUS

Put some "scorpions" in someone's tight shoes or boots. Place the "scorpions" deep into the toe box. When they force their foot into the shoe they will feel the maximum sting of the "scorpion".

SALTING REVENGE

I was both the victim and victimizer to this long running gag. It is old and simple but still so damn funny. This works better with hungover roommates or hard sleepers who wake up groggy and head to the fridge for their favorite drink. All you have to do is pour salt into their favorite morning beverage. Sit back and watch the fun when they take a huge gulp and then spit it all over the floor and walls.

Revenge Idea Upgrades

EVIL PRANK BONUS

This can also be done with a table salt shaker. Just unscrew the cap and place it back on top. When the victim salts their food the whole top comes off and the entire shaker dumps out. You can also take the pepper shaker and fill the top with salt so the victim cannot see it. Unscrew the cap and a bunch of salt and pepper will spill out and ruin the victim's food.

GETTING EVEN BONUS

Salting is also fun to do to toothpaste and mouthwash. You can also salt to someone's milk, alcohol or tea. Salt can also be added to leftovers, breakfast cereal or pizza.

Another great use for salt in to salt somebody's lawn. Mix the salt with water and fill water balloons. You can do a drive by from a car and quickly attack someone's lawn. This will leave large polka dots of dead grass.

You can put salt water in a spray bottle and write a message in the lawn as well. In a few days the message will appear written in dead grass and you will be long gone from the crime scene.

GETTING SERIOUS REVENGE BONUS

Why add salt when you can add eye drops to someone's drink? Be careful with this prank and don't overdo it unless they deserve it. All it should take is a squeeze or three to give a person awful digestive problems.

FIRECRACKER REVENGE

The Firecracker Revenge is a safe prank to use on your house mates. Setting firework traps for your roommates to stumble onto is an old and celebrated tradition that goes back to our country's founding fathers. I am sure Sam Adams used these against John Adams all the time. The easiest traps to set are the string-pull kind. If you are not familiar with what a sting-pull firecracker is let me explain it a little better. This is a firecracker with a long string hanging out on each end. When you pull the strings hard the fire cracker blows up. These are great fun to tie onto your roommate's door knob. What you will want to do to set this trap is to tie the string around the door knob. Pin the other string down by tying it tightly to a well anchored tack pushed hard into the door frame. It will be a fun way to help your hung over or groggy roommate wake up.

Revenge Idea Upgrades

EVIL PRANK BONUS

Fun Snaps are another firecracker that provide tons of entertainment. Let me explain what they are. Fun Snaps are little white balls of paper with powder inside. They make a surprisingly loud pop when they are thrown or stepped on. Lay these all over the bathroom floor, when they get stepped on in such a small room they should be quite noisy.

GETTING EVEN BONUS

We had tons of fun with this old trick in college. I don't smoke and people smoking next to me or in my house drive me crazy. We had a girl on the rugby team that always insisted on smoking. I would steal a pack of cigarettes from her unguarded purse and plant small firecracker sticks called cigarette bangs in the end of the cigarettes. These are sold in a small pack of 10 and say "Exploding Cigarette Bangs".

We would laugh so hard when she would pull out a cigarette at a party and it would blow up in her face. We ruined tons of her cigarettes over the years and made her very paranoid about smoking.

GETTING SERIOUS REVENGE BONUS

One of the funniest ways to use the firecracker prank is to combine the string pull firecracker and fun snaps. Use the string pull as a tripwire and then lay fun snaps all over the floor. The victim will walk out of their room and hear something blow up on their feet. They will jump and run out of their room and step all over the fun snaps on the floor. For the best results when using the Firecracker Revenge pranks, make sure to set the trap in the bathroom and unscrew the light bulb.

CAR PRANKS AND REVENGE

Some people really love their cars so you will want to be careful when selecting a victim. Some people name their cars, protect their cars and use their cars as part of their identity. These are the funniest people to screw with. With victims like this you will want to be anonymous.

One friendly, silly way is put post it notes on every inch of it. Another one of the classic ways to do this is to paste a rude bumper sticker on their car. You should find one that says "honk if you're gay" or "I hate cops". Use your imagination and have some fun. It also cheeses people off if you put their opposite political party on their car.

Revenge Idea Upgrades

EVIL PRANK BONUS

It is also fun to trick your victim into thinking something is really wrong with his car. One of the funniest things to do is to use the old classic Exhaust Whistle Gag. You put this small device in the exhaust pipe and it whistles like mad.

Another way to do this is to tie some empty cans underneath the undercarriage. You will want to tie them deep under the car so the victim can't see them. This will make a hell of a racket on a bumpy road and the victim will think something major is wrong with their car.

GETTING EVEN BONUS

Plant Fun Snaps under all the tires. When these things go off the victim will think something is wrong with their car. Combine the fun snaps with putting a condom around the exhaust pipe. The condom will inflate and blow up.

GETTING SERIOUS REVENGE BONUS

Steal your housemate's keys and pop the hood of their car. You can buy a special firecracker made to fake a car fire. It will smoke like crazy and mimic a fire under the hood. If you want to be a complete jerk stuff a bunch of bananas in the tail pipe too. This causes the oxygen sensor to think there is something wrong and the car will run badly. If you are lucky it will stall out while the smoke bomb is going off under the hood.

CEILING FAN REVENGE

Ceiling fans can be great fun to use as traps. They are a great way to distribute collateral damage to everyone in the room. Of course the old classics are to use confetti or glitter and place it on the top of the fan blades. When the fan is turned on the confetti or glitter will be thrown everywhere. I prefer to use glitter. You can buy a bag of glitter very cheap and when it sprays all over the room the victim will never be able to get it completely cleaned up. Glitter is just so messy and hard to get up. If you don't believe me just ask an adult entertainer how hard glitter is to clean up.

Revenge Idea Upgrades

EVIL PRANK BONUS

Another classic way to do this is load the tops of the fan blades with coins. When the fan turns on and gets some speed going, it will dump the coins everywhere. Warning these coins can really hurt if the fan gets enough speed going.

GETTING EVEN BONUS

If you want to be more malicious, you can use open ketchup packs or tacks on top of the fan blades.

You can also put anything on the blades that would be a real stinky. Try taping small sardines or meat to the top of the fan blades. You will need to distribute the weight evenly so the blades still spin normal.

Another way to screw with the victim is spray fox scent on the light bulb. After the bulb heats up the fan will blow the nasty funk everywhere. The victim will never figure out where the smell is coming from.

GETTING SERIOUS REVENGE BONUS

If you want to be a jerk and destroy someone's room use small plastic cups of liquid. Now of course you can use water and give your victim an indoor shower. If you want to be completely foul you can use other liquids. Fill the cups with dye, sewage water or pee, and really piss them off!

COSMETIC REVENGE

Screwing with people's cosmetics is a time honored tradition that probably dates back to our forefathers. I would like to believe that somebody played a trick on George Washington's wooden teeth. Let's start with the safe pranks: toothpaste and mouth wash are one of the easiest items to attack. Switch the hemorrhoid cream with the toothpaste. It works great on groggy people. Or just simply adding salt is a great way to mess with toothpaste and mouthwash.

Revenge Idea Upgrades

EVIL PRANK BONUS

Hot sauce in the toothpaste or mouthwash is also a fun prank. If you use a sauce hot enough, the victim will spit it out all over the mirror.

GETTING EVEN BONUS

Another classic is to mess with the shower head. You probably remember seeing this in movies. In one old movie they filled the shower head with blue dye and stained the victim. I have never tried this because I figured it would burn someone's eyes, but I have used the less painful version of this prank with drink mix packs. Unscrew the shower head, pour in as many blue drink mix packs that will fit. Screw the head back in place. The victim will be hit with blue-stained water and it is also a gross, sticky mess.

GETTING SERIOUS REVENGE BONUS

Screwing with shampoo and hair gel can be pretty evil as well. You can scale it down by putting ketchup or drink mix packs in shampoo. If you really want to be a jerk then attack the hair gel. Put glue inside the hair gel. Screw the cap back on so the glue won't dry out. When they run the gel through their hair it will quickly become a sticky tangled mess. Most likely they will have to cut the hair out.

BED REVENGE

You can have loads of fun screwing with your roommate's bed. There are tons of pranks you can do with a bed that run the gamut. You can do a silly little joke or get serious payback. We will start with one classic that we used on each other as kids. In fact even my best friends in college did this to me monthly and I still thought it was funny every time. I am referring to the Short Sheet prank.

Here is how it works. You sneak into the bedroom and pull the sheet off. Fold the sheet in half so it creates a pocket facing the pillows. Tuck the folded sheet under the bed, Cover the sheet with a comforter so it can't be seen. The victim's feet get trapped in the sheet pocket and they can't get under their covers.

Revenge Idea Upgrades

EVIL PRANK BONUS

The bed can also be wrapped in plastic wrap or tin foil. This is annoying as hell to clean up if you do it well.

GETTING EVEN BONUS

You can also unscrew the legs on the bed frame and just balance the bed on it. When the victim gets in the bed, it will slide off the legs and hit the floor. This is not too dangerous, but it should scare the hell out of the victim.

If this is too much work you can stick a few empty cans under the legs and it will cause the bed to drop.

GETTING SERIOUS REVENGE BONUS

This will really piss off your roommate. Take a bucket of water or any other fluid of choice and throw it on the mattress, it will stay damp for days and even start to stink. Your roommate will have to sleep on the couch or floor until it dries.

KITCHEN REVENGE

The kitchen can be a place of great fun, as there are so many appliances to booby trap. The easiest thing is to create an avalanche in the freezer. Tape the automatic ice maker bar in the down position so it continually makes ice. This is best to do before a vacation. It will take at least a weekend for the freezer to fill up.

Revenge Idea Upgrades

EVIL PRANK BONUS

You can use the old classic called the water sprayer trap. Just tape down the handle on the sprayer and aim it across the sink. When someone turns on the water they will get sprayed in the face.

GETTING EVEN BONUS

This revenge idea is one of my favorites that I invented. Get a compact disc and put it in a microwave, open the microwave and tape the CD to the inside ceiling of the microwave. Most people will never look around inside of a microwave to see it. When someone starts the microwave the silicon in the disc will put on a huge light show of sparks. It is harmless to the microwave but it should scare the hell out of the victim.

GETTING SERIOUS REVENGE BONUS

This is also a classic my brother pulled on me once. Take a few firecrackers and stick them in the oven, make sure the wicks are touching the heating element. When someone preheats the oven there will be a deafening pop. If you don't care about burn marks inside the oven substitute a pack of jumping jacks and watch the impressive light show.

Chapter 3
COLLEGE PRANKS

Pulling pranks on others makes college a whole lot more bearable. After all college students' lives are so hectic. A student's life is hard when you live on bulk, cheap noodles and ketchup packs you ripped off from the local taco joint. It is so stressful to get drunk at 10 am, skip all your classes and watch old 70's sitcoms. Yep, life is very tough for the young college student.

The only way to alleviate this stress is to pull pranks. This is the chapter of the book where I have listed some of the tricks I pulled off when I was in college. There are also much more disgusting pranks I pulled off in college under the Very Gross Pranks chapter. Be warned, don't go to that chapter unless you love low brow humor.

A word of warning, it is always better to do these revenge ideas and remain anonymous. Some of these pranks will bring down a terrible wrath if you're caught and will start a prank war that can last for years. Make sure you pick a victim that is too chicken to fight back or remain invisible during your attacks.

IMPRISONING PRANKS

Locking people in their own room can provide hours of amusement. The old standby prank is to just take the door knob off and reverse it so the unlocking mechanism is now outside of the room. Most people won't ever notice it has been reversed until it is too late. Simply set the lock mechanism to lock mode and just wait for the person to shut the door behind them when they go into their room.

This will work when you are not even home so you can play ignorant.

Prank Idea Upgrades

EVIL PRANK BONUS

If you don't want to deal with switching the lock use this old classic. Wipe petroleum jelly on the inside door knob. It is very hard to turn the knob and as an added bonus the victim gets petroleum jelly all over their hands.

GETTING EVEN BONUS

You can also use the oldest classic I know. Hell, my grandfather showed me this trick and he said his dad showed it to him, so who knows how old this is. It is the penny wedge. It takes two people to make this work. Make sure the victim is in their room sleeping. The first person pushes hard on the door and the second person wedges pennies right near the lock and the door frame. Try to stack about 3-5 pennies in the gap to get a very tight fit. The forced pressure from the pennies on the lock doesn't let it work. Oh here is a warning by the way, it is a total bitch to get those pennies back out.

GETTING SERIOUS REVENGE BONUS

This is the funniest form of the Imprisoning Prank, if you can pull it off. Go to a dorm hallway and see if you can find 2 doors that swing inward and are across from each other you can have some real fun. Wait for both victims to be in their rooms. Get a strong rope or cable and tie both of the door knobs together. You must pull this rope or cable very tight all the way across the hall. When the victim tries to open their door the rope or cable won't let the door swing inward. Even better, if you leave a little slack in the rope and knock on both peoples doors. They will be able to crack the door a little and see each other trapped. If you very lucky they will get into a tug of war with their doors.

Dog Swap Prank

This is by far one of the funniest and light-hearted pranks I ever pulled off. I love dogs so I would never do anything mean to one, but they do make great props in pranks. Back in college many people owned dogs but they never paid very good attention to them. Well, some guys on the rugby team had a black lab in one house and some other ruggers had a similar looking dog. I snuck in, right in the middle of the day, took a leash and stole the dog. I broke in the other house and stole the look-alike dog. I swapped the dogs and put them into each other's house. A day or two went by before someone was sitting and scratching the dog's stomach, when they noticed their dog became a boy.

Prank Idea Upgrades

EVIL PRANK BONUS

Switch two dogs for one. Try to find two dogs of the same breed that you are planning on switching. See how long it takes before someone suddenly realizes the dog has cloned itself.

GETTING EVEN BONUS

Use the same idea as above but set up a little dog cloning lab, complete with beakers and notes on cloning in his dog bed.

GETTING SERIOUS REVENGE BONUS

Take the Dog Swap Prank to a higher level. Take a random dog from a friend's house, dognap it and leave a note saying, "Went out on the town. Be back in a few - Rover". Then take the dog and drop it in the victim's house when nobody is there. Leave a note where everyone can see it saying "Dear roommates, I got a new dog. I will explain later". Don't sign a name on it and watch all the roommates think it is the others' new dog. After a day or two you leave a note at the dognapping house with the address of where there dog has been residing. Note should read, "Dude, I met these bitches and they took me back to their dog house. I need a ride home I am at (victims address)". Never tell either house it was you and enjoy them trying to figure out who would do such a silly prank.

FIRE SALE PRANKS

Again, I fell victim to this one after toilet papering my friend's house. He retaliated a week later with the fire sale. Basically this can work for many items your victim owns which can be seen by the public. My friends did this prank to my first car, a 1985 Chrysler LeBaron. All they did was put a sign on it saying, "must sell today, only $50, runs great". Needless to say only minutes later some poor schmuck saw it, brought his whole family to see it and take it for a test drive. When he knocked on my door and I answered I had no idea what he was talking about. The man kept insisting that a maroon Chrysler LeBaron was for sale in front of my house for only $50. After repeating telling him that I really had no idea what he was talking about I shut the door on him.

He pounded on the door and adamantly insisted I go take a look with him. I went outside and lo and behold there was the sign. I instantly knew who did it because the sign also had green shamrocks drawn on the corners. Then, I saw a car load of my Irish friends howling their heads off as the spun out from behind a bush in their car. Needless to say the poor guy who thought it was for sale was super pissed and stormed off.

Prank Idea Upgrades

EVIL PRANK BONUS

Try this on your children's bike, skateboard or possessions they won't put away.

GETTING EVEN BONUS

Put a sign on an item before midnight that reads, "Must sell tonight! Only $50. PLEASE KNOCK ON DOOR, I WILL BE UP LATE NIGHT WAITING". Sit back and enjoy watching some schmuck wake your tired and dazed friend at 1 A.M. to buy his car.

GETTING SERIOUS REVENGE BONUS

Wait until you know your victim is leaving town. Place a sign on the vehicle or boat that says "MUST SELL TODAY, I WILL BE RIGHT BACK, PLEASE WAIT". Make sure you leave all your victims phone numbers. Then sit back and enjoy all the calls from the incredibly pissed off people who have been waiting for hours to buy it.

P.S . - To enjoy the Fire Sale prank all weekend, make sure to glue the sign down to the windshield so the victim can't tell the pissed off buyers to take it off. If they do tear it off just replace it as soon as they leave.

MAIL PRANKS

Find out your victim's house address or dorm P.O. Box. Then for an entire week call every single commercial on TV and ask for information to be sent to them. I mean everything from the D.R. Mower to diabetes testing supplies and hover rounds. You will be impressed with how much stuff you can order in just one week if you watch enough different stations. Don't forget to order all the erectile dysfunction and herpes medicine information you can get.

Prank Idea Upgrades

EVIL PRANK BONUS

Try to go to your local book stores and pull out as many magazine inserts as possible. Take an afternoon and fill them all out, mark them "Bill me later".

GETTING EVEN BONUS

Sign them up for Scientology information. They will continue sending your victim mail for the rest of their life. There is no way to get the mail to stop.

You can also sign them up for the Book of Mormon. They will send your victim information for years.

While you're add it sign them up for all the religious information you can find. Flood their mail book with everything from voodoo to Islam.

GETTING SERIOUS REVENGE BONUS

Sign the wife or daughter up for planned parenthood or adoption option programs. You can also get a magazine insert to gay magazine and order them a subscription. Try to find one with a great title like BEAR'S LIFE or DYKE.

If your victim is gay it is just as funny and embarrassing to send them religious magazines that disapprove of homosexuality. Sign your gay friend up for Jerry Fallwell's newsletter.

PET MAKEOVER PRANKS

This is great prank to do to someone in college or the office who owns a pet they are crazy about. When I was in college, a girl there was a rugby player that went everywhere with her dog. The dog was super sweet so I didn't want to do anything that would ever harm the dog. Breaking in her house was super easy because in college nobody ever locked all their doors, especially when they lived with roommates. I dognapped her dog and left this note behind. "Dear Nicky, I went out on the town dancing. I will be back later tonight." Then I went to the thrift store and bought a very small '70's disco shirt and some '70's accessories. I dressed the dog up and tied the shirt down to fit right. I opened the shirt chest and put the butterfly collar up. I also adorned the canine with some proper '70's bling and little baby shoes spray painted gold I had tied on her paws. The dog was surprising good natured about all this and enjoyed the attention. I sneaked over later that night and quietly opened the back door and let the dog back in. I stayed outside until I heard hysterical laugher and took off. As usual I denied the incident when questioned.

Prank Idea Upgrades

EVIL PRANK BONUS

The Pet Makeover Revenge can also be done with a cat. A word of warning, very few cats will put up with you dressing them so if you try it, you better be ready to get the hell scratched out of you. Another fun thing to do to with cats and small little furry toy dogs is to use this prank. Get a big can of petroleum jelly and spread it thick all over the pet's coat. The pet will track it everywhere in the house and the owner will have to spend a good amount of time scrubbing it out of their coats.

GETTING EVEN BONUS

You can use somebody's cat to rearrange a Christmas tree. I saw this done by my friend's wife who got very drunk. She picked up the cat and dropped it in the rugby house's Christmas tree. The cat climbed around the whole tree attacked the ornaments. The cat did very thorough job and threw every ornament on the floor. It was hilarious to watch and the cat seemed to really enjoy his work. Needless to say the owner of the Christmas tree was not at all pleased.

GETTING SERIOUS REVENGE BONUS

This is another funny Pet Makeover prank. I pulled this gag on a teammate's dog on April Fool's night. This trick only works on light colored pets like white or tan. I dognapped my friends Dalmatian and dyed him pink. Dogs have sensitive skin so you can't use any chemicals. The best way to do this is to take a couple of red or blue drink mix packs. Basically, you're looking for colored sugar water. This way when the pet tries to lick it off it won't hurt him. I returned the dog later that night but he stayed pink for over a week.

If you're really daring you can shave a message to your victim into the dog's coat.

DRUNK PRANKS

Messing with drunks is a time honored college tradition. Inevitably, a college victim will drink way too much and present an easy target. You need to be very stealthy if the victim has friends around. Most of the time, you can recruit their friends to be on in the prank if you buy them off with a beer. The simplest thing to do to somebody who is passed out is to create art on them. Get a real thick permanent marker and start writing messages on their face. "Fart monger" or "I love Gay Men" are always choice. I remember there was a girl rugby player we used to draw on all the time. One time I drew Elvis side burns on her and she went to the dining hall in the morning without looking in a mirror. She wore the chops all day to classes too, it was so funny.

Prank Idea Upgrades

EVIL PRANK BONUS

Another classic prank is to shave off just one eyebrow. I also have seen a guy with long hair pass out and my brother's friends' cut one side of the long hair and glued the cut off hair to the other side. The victim loved his long hair and was super pissed. Even to this day, nobody will admit they had anything to do with the prank because the victim is still mad.

GETTING EVEN BONUS

One thing about drinking is it makes you have to pee like crazy. You can be very mean and super glue the victim's zipper. When the victim stumbles drunk to the bathroom they won't be able to figure out how to get out of their pants.

GETTING SERIOUS REVENGE BONUS

Lots of fun can be done with duct tape and some strong friends. Simply drag out the body and duct tape the victim to a wall or tree. Make sure to get pictures and be careful not to be recognized.

COLLEGE SEX PRANKS

Some of the funniest pranks we ever did in college in involved nudity and sexual jokes. This is not a new idea by any means. Jokes that involved nudity have been making people laugh since there was the invention of college. It can even go back as far as the Romans. The Romans frequently drew obscene sexual graffiti to get revenge on their politicians and popular figures.

The simplest nude prank that still is very funny is streaking. Streaking really came into its own in the '60s when countless people were doing it at public events. Even though it is harder to pull off these days, it is still a very funny prank if you have the balls to try it.

Prank Idea Upgrades

EVIL PRANK BONUS

Of course streaking a graduation earns you extra kudo points. It was a fairly common prank to be naked under your graduation robe and flash the crowd when you got your diploma.

GETTING EVEN BONUS

Embarrassing nudity was always the consequence of losing a drinking game to your fellow rugby teammates. As time went on the nudity pranks got funnier and funnier. It started with streaking a random dorm hall to standing in the campus fountain and pretending to be a naked statue.

One of the funniest nudity pranks I ever saw was when a fellow teammate lost a drinking game and had to go to the local convenience store naked and bring back a napkin. That poor 7-11 was the victim of some sort of nudity every week!

GETTING SERIOUS REVENGE BONUS

Of course the best college sex prank is to ruin your friends chances of hooking up and having sex. I remember when we were coming back from a party and saw a fellow rugby player having sex on the couch in the main room. Of course, we snuck in quietly to interrupt this. One of my teammates sneaked up with a feather and kept tickling his feet from behind the couch. The fellow rugby player having sex knew he was caught but his date didn't. The situation left him in a very uncomfortable spot if he should finish having sex or not.

Anytime you can block your friend from having sex you should. It is always funny!

44

Chapter 4
HIGH SCHOOL
AND SENIOR PRANKS

I really didn't care for high school and could not stand sitting all day in classes I hated. I felt like time was in slow motion for 4 years and couldn't wait to go to college. The only way I kept my sanity was to screw with my classmates, teachers and school. I am proud to say I never got caught for any pranks I did because I carefully laid out my plans ahead of time. I did get Saturday school once for my sarcastic mouth, but to this day I still believe it was worth it. So since you can't express free speech in a government school, stealth prank attacks are your only option.

These pranks are mostly classics that people have been pulling on their high schools for years. There are also some pranks in this section that will be pulled outside of the school. I lumped them in this section because these classic pranks are some of the first pranks a student pulls.

Here is a word of wisdom I want to pass down. High school allows for some great pranks but you really want to remain anonymous. I had many friends in high school who were sloppy and got caught and suspended.

Remember the more people in on the prank the better chance you will get busted. The fewer people in on it, the better off you are. Most of the time you want to do these alone if possible.

Great high school pranks are in a class of their own. Usually, they are large scale pranks and you will need access to the school during evening hours.

COIN PRANKS

Screwing with your school and teachers can help pass the time. Most of the time, school is mind numbing and you need some good pranks to liven things up. Screwing with school property or a teacher can land you in some hot water. You need to remain anonymous and it would be wise to bring a look out with you. Put pennies all over the floor and make bets to see if your teacher is broke enough to pick them up.

Prank Idea Upgrades

EVIL PRANK BONUS

The draw of free money can provide hours of cheap entertainment. This is a very old classic but it is still so funny to watch. Get a few quarters and glue them to the floor. Sit back and count all the students who bend down to get it. We used to really laugh when the teachers would try and pick it up.

GETTING EVEN BONUS

You can also try this in the bathroom. Get some gloves and glue a dollar coin into a urinal or toilet. You will probably have to upgrade to a dollar because it is doubtful they will reach into a toilet for just a quarter. Imagine how mad they will be that they stuck their hand in a toilet only to find the coin is glued down.

GETTING SERIOUS REVENGE BONUS

If you know you got a test you don't want to take or simply you just don't want to go to class then you can use this prank. What you can do is glue coins on doorknob locks to your classroom. If you use fast-drying, extra strong glue you can do this right before your test so your teacher can not get into your classroom.

LOCKER PRANKS

Great fun can be had to somebody who does not protect their locker well. I had a friend of mine who hated screwing with his lock so he secretly left his locker unlocked the whole school year. This was a big mistake, because word got out and we used to do stuff to his locker every other week. Now the classic, of course, is to decorate the locker with porn. Hell, you can just go to the internet and print pictures out to your heart's content. Of course if your victim is homophobic, gay porn should be used. Then when your victim opens their locker everyone will see their dirty gay porn secret.

Prank Idea Upgrades

EVIL PRANK BONUS

You can always add a pad lock to your victim's locker so they can't get in.

You can also take some black paint and paint over the numbers on the lock. The victim won't be able to figure out how to open the lock without numbers.

You can rub ink, petroleum jelly or itching powder all over the locker handle.

GETTING EVEN BONUS

Do they lock their locker and you can't get access? You can still screw with their stuff thanks to the vents they put in the locker door. Get some shaving cream, foam spray or even cheese spray. Basically, you can use any liquid you can get into a spray bottle so use your imagination.

GETTING SERIOUS REVENGE BONUS

Do you want to be a real jerk, spray deer scent or fox pee through the vents. You can buy this in the outdoors section of a superstore. They will never figure out why their locker reeks for a month. The scent will also cling to their belongings. You can also be a real jerk and combine this with some locker ideas from here.

PRANKING OTHER STUDENTS

Sometimes students were more annoying the teachers. We had tons of jack ass students who were a real pain to deal with. Instead of confronting them you will get much more pleasure screwing with them all year. The home work switch is a fun way to get them in trouble. When you get a homework assignment, make an extra fake one that is not only all wrong, but very rude. Be sure to not make it your handwriting. There are two ways to switch the homework. The first is to switch them while everyone is handing them up and the stack comes across your desk. The second way is to wait until after class and get to them when your teacher leaves the stack of homework unguarded.

Free Revenge Ideas Upgrades

EVIL PRANK BONUS

The next way is to put itching powder in locker. Ideally, if you can get access to their back pack, that is where you want to strike. Be careful not to get this stuff on you, it is seriously evil and will cause you terrible irritation.

GETTING EVEN BONUS

Design a bunch of posters of your victim. Try to make them look like child kidnapping ones you see at the post office. Post them all over and listen to the rumors run through school that your victim was kidnapped.

GETTING SERIOUS REVENGE BONUS

Take it a bit further and make a website of your victim. Make an anonymous email account and then go to Myspace or Facebook and make your victim a web page. Have fun with it and make it horrible. Make sure the address gets out and your classmates and they will spread it everywhere. Put some seriously sick stuff so when a school administrator "accidentally" gets the website's address, it will get your victim suspended. You will get totally busted and this page will get traced to you unless you hide your IP address. If you're serious about Pranking Other Students you will need to do this.

PRANKING TEACHERS

I liked most of my teachers in high school, but there were a handful that were nasty people. Since you can't openly tell a teacher to go to hell and stop ruining your life you must strike with stealth. Be sure to remain anonymous. Your teacher will suspect it's you but will never be able to prove it if you do these right. That's the funniest part, that they know it is you but cannot do a damn thing about it.

Sure it was always fun to make a fake magazine ad about your teacher, but these days students need better pranks. First, let us discuss substitute teachers. This is easy; you simply have to act like you're a new foreign student. Have your friend say you speak some obscure Russian dialect. Every time you speak your language, it should be littered with words that sound very similar to cuss words. I would hate to substitute teach, and I really have no idea why anybody would.

Prank Idea Upgrades

EVIL PRANK BONUS

If your teacher is a coffee or tea drinker there is a great prank you can do. You need to do this prank while the coffee or tea is still hot or it won't work right. Distract your teacher and slip in these two types of powder in their hot drink. The first is Belch Powder and the second is Fart Powder.

These powders are downright evil and are just plain mean to do to somebody. The best part about Pranking Teachers this way is your teacher will never have a clue while they got such horrible gas. If you are good at this prank, you can do this to your teachers or parents a few times a week.

GETTING EVEN BONUS

I am not a big fan of government schools. One of the big reasons is because most of the teachers are incompetent and completely lost without their material.

Just watch for awhile and you will see where your teacher using their lesson plans. Most teachers use their lesson plans every year and all of them are in one big folder or laptop. You will need to steal or destroy this folder. If they have a laptop, just format the hard drive and that will erase all their lesson plans. We stole a teacher's lesson plans one year and the teacher was seriously crippled and worthless for the rest of the year.

GETTING SERIOUS REVENGE BONUS

Pranking Teachers with this can get them fired. Take it a bit further and make a website for your teacher. Make up some good rumors about an alternative lifestyle. Photoshop some good pictures of them and their alternative lifestyle. Here is how to set it up. Make an anonymous email account and then go to Myspace or Facebook and make your victim a webpage. If you're serious about Pranking Teachers you need to make sure the webpage address gets out anonymously and your classmates and they will spread it everywhere. Put some seriously sick stuff so the school administrator will fire them when they "accidentally" get the website's address. You will get totally busted and this page will get traced to you unless you hide your IP address. Make sure you hide your IP first before doing anything else.

CLASSIC SENIOR PRANKS

Everyone has heard of most of these pranks but they are still worth mentioning because they are pretty funny. The first involves screwing with a fountain. If your school is dumb enough to have a fountain they might as well paint a bull's eye on it. Fountain pranks have probably been around since the days of Rome. You can dye the water, or fill it with tons of bubble bath. You can use laundry detergent or on Halloween use dry ice to make it bubble and mist. If there is no fountain then you will have to fill the laundry machines or leave a sink running into a bucket of bubble bath.

Prank Idea Upgrades

EVIL PRANK BONUS

A prank that is still funny is to stack all the cafeteria tables on top of each other.

Another Classic Senior Prank worth mentioning, that might be impossible to do these days because heightened school security, is the classic car in the school. It was a very popular prank back in the '70s and '80s but much harder to do now. Basically a group of students would disassemble a car and reassemble somewhere in the school.

GETTING EVEN BONUS

This is a much meaner and more destructive prank that will piss the whole school off. Wait till schools out for the day so nobody will see you. You will need to buy lots of extra strong glue. Go down the halls and glue each dial on the lockers. Don't forget to put glue in the keyholes to. Be sure to wear gloves because this gets very messy and your fingerprints will be everywhere. The next day the entire school will be locked out of their lockers and the administration will have to break the ruined lock off each locker. This will take days before everyone can get their books or assignments out of their locker and will massively disrupt every class.

GETTING SERIOUS REVENGE BONUS

This is also one of the most destructive Classic Senior Pranks that will piss off the whole school, so again you will want to remain anonymous. You will need to get lots of old ground meat. Buy the cheapest stuff you can find and let it age a day or two. Get some gloves and a mask and stuff thin layers of meat into envelops. You will then go to your school on a Friday afternoon when nobody sees you. You want to go on a Friday or before a holiday break to give the meat a few days to rot. Take the thin meat filled envelopes and stick them through the vents on the locker. The meat will heat up, rot, stink and leak all over everybody's stuff in their locker. You would be surprised you don't need much meat to make this work and if you do it before a week long break there will be flies and maggots everywhere.

OLD SCHOOL PRANKS

This is a collection of some of the most famous nostalgic pranks. I am sure you probably know these pranks but if you have never actually done them then you are missing out. These pranks have been around forever because they are just so fun to do. Let me knock the dust off these old classics and bring them back to your devious attention.

Let's start with the classic Soul Train scramble board. If you are too young to not know what Soul Train is then ignore that joke. Basically you find a school or fast food joints sign and rearrange the letters. This can be great fun but it does take impressive word jumble skills.

Prank Idea Upgrades

EVIL PRANK BONUS

Another great prank is to steal all the neighborhood Realtor signs and place them all in the victim's yards. If you get lucky you will find some "It's a girl" signs with a stork on it. Those are always funny if you can get them.

GETTING EVEN BONUS

Forking a yard is an old classic but still very funny. Buy a ton of cheap plastic forks and stick them all over the yard like they just grew over night.

GETTING SERIOUS REVENGE BONUS

Of course the granddaddy of them all is toilet papering or rolling a house. It seems so simple but it is a complete pain to clean up. You will want to buy the cheapest stuff you can find and then wait until a rainy night. If the toilet paper gets too wet it becomes impossible to remove.

Don't forget to toilet paper all the cars in the driveway too. Roll the mailbox, doorway, and mulch and then wet it down if with the victim's own hose.

Childhood Pranks

This section really takes me back! Some of the funniest stuff is the silliest. Probably the first pranks a young prankster learns is the ring and run. I think that was my first prank or it might have been rolling a house a.k.a. tee peeing a house. I want to talk about some other great classics, let's start with these.

Prank Idea Upgrades

EVIL PRANK BONUS

The crime scene or playing dead is one of my favorites. Basically you round up a group of friends and pour fake blood on yourselves. Then you all lay around the front yard or the sidewalks so cars can see you. Hide until a car drives by and chase one of your friends with a fake knife and "stab" them to death on the side walk, then "stab" yourself to death.

Cars will fall for this and some people will freak out. If you do get busted have a camcorder around so you can say you're making a slasher movie.

By the way if you do film this prank send us a clip please! See the site at:

http://TheBestPrankBookEver.LupoLit.com/

GETTING EVEN BONUS

You can also due this prank with a zombie theme. If your friends are good with some theater make up you can really have some fun. Wait for a car to come by and have the zombies catch and eat you. Have them surround you and throw blood and raw meat into the air.

GETTING SERIOUS REVENGE BONUS

If you are broke you and your friends can always pull the invisible rope prank. You will divide your friends so half are on one side of the road and half are on the other. Set up like your all holding one big rope and having a tug of war.

You will all crouch down until a car gets close. Then you will all stand up and act like you're pulling a rope.

This confuses the driver of the car because they see everyone pulling a rope but they don't see a rope. They will usually slowdown or stop. When they do you all drop the fake rope and laugh and point at the driver. This is such a funny childhood prank to pull.

Chapter 5
GIRLFRIENDS REVENGE

Nothing inspires such angry payback as a woman scorned. The famous quote "Hell has no fury like a woman scorned" says it all. It feels great to get even with a lying cheating jerk.

This section of the website is designed to help you bring down the fury on your victim. If you have been scorned and want payback your at the right place. We offer some revenge ideas that run the gambit. You can pull some silly pranks to get them back or you can get much nastier. If you're looking for pranks that won't get you in trouble or possibly arrested there are tons elsewhere in this book. Take your time and look around. The ideas in this chapter will be a little meaner and hopefully let you get some degree of revenge.

GAY DATING REVENGE

This is a classic payback that you will want to use. Although it is an older idea it still is very funny. If your ex is homophobic it is self explanatory. If your victim is gay then replace this revenge idea with straight Christian dating sites. You want to stay anonymous on this one, trust me. First things first, you need to hide your IP address. For the readers who are not tech savvy let me explain. Your computer has an address that leaves itself on everything you look at on the net. Tech savvy people can trace anything you do back to your IP address and find you. You will need to hide this first before you start your attacks. The best way to do this is to use this program. This program is the best bang for the buck and the only one I trust. You will need it for many more of these pranks so I suggest you take a look.

http://www.hide-my-ip.com/?id=469

The way to start this prank is to do some surfing and find some gay dating sites. If you can't find a free one then go to your town's Craigslist website. If you don't know what Craigslist is, it is a free classified online newspaper.

Now that you know where to place an ad you need an anonymous email. Go to Gmail, Yahoo or Hotmail and make one in the ex's name. Now, simply write an ad and post it.

Revenge Idea Upgrades

EVIL PRANK BONUS

If you use the Craigslist technique you will more than likely get flagged when the victim founds out. You will just have to keep posting new ads. To get the most out of the Craigslist technique you want to put up any compromising pictures you have of your ex and put all the details including their home and office phone number and their address. You will have to disguise the info to get it up, but look at the other ads to figure out how to do this.

GETTING EVEN BONUS

Start responding to the gay pick up emails you get and save them. You can always post them later in this other prank Then send a picture of your ex and say you want to meet up at their office or home. Hopefully, you know your ex's routine and send the gay interest to their house or to their work. Be sure to send all the people you have been corresponding with to your ex's house around the same time. This will really piss off all parties at your ex.

GETTING SERIOUS REVENGE BONUS

Why not take it a step further and post a prostitution ad on Craigslist. Go to the erotic services area and you will see prostitution ads. Why not put one up for your ex. If you're real lucky the police check those ads all the time and they might contact your ex. If you did not hide your IP address, you will be sorry when the cops coming looking for you.

WEBSITE REVENGE

This is a prank that is fun to pull on your friends, coworkers and ex's. This revenge can be light hearted or just a plain evil prank. You need to ask yourself how mean you want to go with this website revenge. If you plan on getting very nasty then let me say this.

You want to stay anonymous on this one, trust me. First things first, you need to hide your IP address. (see link just above this section title)

If you plan on just doing this to do a friendly prank you don't need to hide your IP. If you want to have real fun then I strongly urge you to buy that program and install it before you start the rest of this prank.

You will need an email address first. Go to Gmail, Yahoo or Hotmail and make an account for your victim. The next thing to do is set up an anonymous website. There are many free web hosting sites. And Geocities is a yahoo site, so you can just use the new Yahoo email to make it quickly.

Just use the templates that Yahoo provides and make it easy on yourself. If you're feeling nice just put up silly pictures and make their interests a bunch of childish things. Say their interests are unicorns, Beanie Babies and stuff like that.

Revenge Idea Upgrades

EVIL PRANK BONUS

If you want to get meaner then post unflattering pictures where the victim looks fat or stupid and send out an email to your friends saying look what I just found.

GETTING EVEN BONUS

Still want meaner? Post your victim's website with an obviously gay overtone. Make it pink and put links to a bunch of gay organizations. Combine this with the Gay Dating and have some real fun.

GETTING SERIOUS REVENGE BONUS

Take it a step further by exposing their sick fetishes. Photoshop in some leather hoods and some bondage and viola. Then make sure you post your new sites address all over the victim's town's Criagslist page.

To really get the most mileage out of website revenge, send some anonymous emails to the victim's friends and family. Just say, "I was just surfing this morning and came across this sight, have you seen it?" or "I can't believe this is Jim's web page, did you know he had this perverted side to him?"

That should start the rumor mill and the victim's friends and family will spread the address of the web page like a virus.

UNDERWEAR AND CONDOM REVENGE

If you have a house mate, ex or friend and can get access to their underwear you can have enormous amounts of fun. Let's start with the classics. Capture a CLEAN pair you know they will be wearing soon and turn it inside out. Get some numbing sports cream and put it in the crotch area. You don't need much put it on lightly. You don't want it too greasy or slimy or the victim will find it. The victim won't notice it at first until they sweat a little. As soon as the moisture and oxygen hit, it will really start burning.

Revenge Idea Upgrades

EVIL PRANK BONUS

The other classic of course is to put itching powder in the underwear. Everyone has heard of this trick but it is still just an awful thing to do to someone. This particular itching powder is just plain vicious. Be careful not to get it on yourself.

GETTING EVEN BONUS

Messing with a condom is a pretty evil thing to do to somebody, but I am sure some jerks deserve it. Steal the victim's condom. You will also need a syringe to do this prank. You can load the syringe with sports balm or itching powder.

You must use a very small amount or the victim will know. Stick the needle into the condom package and inject a small amount of it in. If you also what to get the victims sex partner inject both sides of the condom package.

GETTING SERIOUS REVENGE BONUS

Underwear And Condom Revenge can also be done with hot sauce. Endorphin Rush hot sauce is some of the hottest hot sauce around. A note on this hot sauce, there are many hotter but if you go past 250,000 Scoville units it will probably burn the skin permanently, so you really don't even want to touch this stuff.

The way I discovered this stuff is through a group of my best friends. Basically, some of them got it on their hands and had sex later or used the bathroom and touched themselves. They described it as a horrible pain that would not stop burning. This stuff is just pure evil to put in condoms, underwear or toilet wipes.

GETTING AN EX FIRED

Getting An Ex Fired is pretty hardcore revenge. Sometimes, your ex is such a jerk they deserve full blown payback. We will examine some ways just to make them the butt of their office's jokes. Let's start with making them uncomfortable at work. For the first prank you will need to find a very unflattering picture of them. Then find a company that makes a life sized cardboard clone of them.

Have the clone delivered to their lobby for everyone to see when they come in. If the picture is funny enough their coworkers will never let them live it down.

Revenge Idea Upgrades

EVIL PRANK BONUS

If you want to step it up a level then do this prank. Before you do this, you will need to hide your IP address or you can easily get busted. You will need this program before doing this prank.

Get your victim's work phone number to the receptionist and the office's address. Now Google home based business info and visit those sites. You want to sign your victim up to ones that want your phone number and personal info. Only give them the victim's work phone number not your victims home number. You are looking for ones that say they will contact you after you enter your information.

What happens is these information collecting websites sell the info to telemarketers. Now if you do this on about 20 pages, the receptionist will get nonstop calls from telemarketers looking for your victim. This will go on for weeks possibly months. Just keep giving the victim's information out on these sites every few weeks. As a bonus do the same thing to their cell phone and all these calls will burn up their minutes and drive them crazy.

GETTING EVEN BONUS

If you have access to their work email you can also cause tons of problems doing the technique listed above. Hopefully their email is monitored and their boss will be tipped off that the victim is looking to start a home business, which leads right into the next revenge idea:

GETTING SERIOUS REVENGE BONUS

If you're really interested in Getting An Ex Fired you will want to find out who their main workplace competitor is. You will want to construct a fake rejection letter from the main competitor. You will want to send the letter to their work with no name listed so the receptionist will open it. The letter should say something like, "Dear (victim's name), After careful consideration we have to reject your application. We have to admit, your offer to bring over all your accounts from (victim's company) and information was very tempting but we were advised by or attorneys that this would be highly unethical. We are sorry and we want to wish you good luck in your job search." If you have access you can also leave this letter in the fax or copy machine for a fellow employee to "stumble" across.

Be sure if you do this to not leave fingerprints on the envelope or paper. You will also want to mail it from a mailbox that is not in your neighborhood.

FAKE PREGNANCY REVENGE

This by far is one of the meanest pranks you can pull on an ex. This revenge has been around for thousands of years. Women have used fake pregnancy to control and terrify men since pregnancy existed.

Women have faked being pregnant to keep men in their life and manipulate them to do their bidding. A fake pregnancy is a very powerful weapon in your revenge arsenal.

A fake pregnancy can also be used to keep a man away. If you have a man who just won't leave you alone you can scare the hell out of him with the idea of responsibility. To most young or irresponsible men nothing is more unattractive the idea of being a father.

Revenge Idea Upgrades

EVIL PRANK BONUS

Fake pregnancy revenge depends on your situation. If you want the man to go away you will want to let one of your friends pass the rumor to him. Have your friend say you're pregnant and you're not sure who the dad is. The reaction of most men will be waiting and see. They will completely disappear and leave you alone if they are unsure if it is theirs.

GETTING EVEN BONUS

If you want to use the pregnancy to keep a man around you definitely want to tell them you are 100% sure it is theirs. You will have a good 3-5 months before you are supposed to be showing. This will buy you a few months more to work things out. Just lie and say you went to the doctors and everything is good.

GETTING SERIOUS REVENGE BONUS

Women who really commit to doing this get all their friends in on it. The even send fake belly and ultrasound pictures. When you done torturing him you can fake a miscarriage or just disappear and tell him absolutely nothing. If you want to rub it in his face tell him you faked it and laugh at him.

IDEAS ON RUINING HIS WEDDING

Does your victim deserve to have their wedding ruined? Want to try and break up a wedding because you the person they are marrying is all wrong for them? Do you think your best friend is marrying a gigolo and you need to let them know? Perhaps you just want the victim to suffer because they are such a horrible person. I will give you a few ideas on how to get revenge by destroying the victim's wedding day.

The first idea is to try and strike before they get married. Convince the future spouse that the victim is unfaithful by spreading rumors using false emails and dating sites. Create a profile for your victim and try and start hitting on anyone that will talk to you. Give them your victim's name, phone of the future spouse and address.

Revenge Idea Upgrades

EVIL PRANK BONUS

Make the guests hate the marrying couple. Find out some of the people on the invite list and send them rude invitations. Suggest the gift they should bring and mention they should not come if they cannot afford to bring it.

Pretend to be the victim and go change their registry to nothing but outrageously expensive gifts.

GETTING EVEN BONUS

Find out all the details you can about the wedding. Wait until a week before and make some calls pretending to be the victim. Cancel their reception hall, band, photographer, cake, and so on. If you're lucky, the victim won't find out until it is too late. Even if the victim finds out and repairs some of the damage it will cause massive stress and confusion on their wedding day.

Another idea is to hire an advertising plane that can pull a banner to fly over the outdoor wedding. Have it say something like, "Don't marry that cheat!"

GETTING SERIOUS REVENGE BONUS

If you cannot stop the wedding you can wreck their honeymoon by canceling it. Cancel their flight and hotel. Anonymously report their car to the police and say they are acting like newlyweds to smuggle drugs across the border.

If none of this works and you can't wreck the wedding, you can send out rude thank you notes to the guest. Thank the guest for their cheap gifts.

Chapter 6
BOYFRIENDS REVENGE

These revenge ideas run the gambit depending on how mean you want to get. Sometimes you need a minor prank that is just enough to send your ex a message without getting you in trouble. Other times you want to get downright nasty and ruin your ex's life like they ruined yours.

Read this whole book and find a prank that is just right to use in your situation. Be very careful, and I highly recommend you remain anonymous.

No victim is more dangerous to get even with then a pissed off ex girlfriend. Sure, posting an embarrassing ex girlfriend picture is fun to do, just make sure you follow all the recommended ways to hide your identity. Most importantly you need to find a good program to hide your IP address before you post anything.

LESBIAN/BI DATING REVENGE

This is a classic payback that you will want to use. Although it is an older idea it still is very funny. If your ex is homophobic it is self explanatory. If your victim is gay then replace this revenge idea with straight Christian dating sites. You want to stay anonymous on this one, trust me. First things first, you need to hide your IP address. For the readers who are not tech savvy let me explain. Your computer has an address that leaves itself on everything you look at on the net. Tech savvy people can trace anything you do back to your IP address and find you. You will need to hide this first before you start your attacks.

The way to start this prank is to do some surfing and find some gay dating sites. If you can't find a free one then go to your town's Craigslist website. If you don't know what Craigslist is, it is a free classified online newspaper.

Now that you know where to place an ad you need an anonymous email. Go to Gmail, Yahoo or Hotmail and make one in the ex's name. Now, simply write an ad and post it.

Revenge Idea Upgrades

EVIL PRANK BONUS

If you use the Craigslist technique you will more than likely get flagged when the victim founds out. You will just have to keep posting new ads. To get the most out of the Craigslist technique you want to put up any compromising pictures you have of your ex and put all the details including their home and office phone number and their address. You will have to disguise the info to get it up, but look at the other ads to figure out how to do this.

GETTING EVEN BONUS

Start responding to the gay pick up emails you get and save them. You can always post them later in this other prank Then send a picture of your ex and say you want to meet up at their office or home. Hopefully, you know your ex's routine and send the gay interest to their house or to their work. Be sure to send all the people you have been corresponding with to your ex's house around the same time. This will really piss off all parties at your ex.

GETTING SERIOUS REVENGE BONUS

Why not take it a step further and post a prostitution ad on Craigslist. Go to the erotic services area and you will see prostitution ads. Why not put one up for your ex. If you're real lucky the police check those ads all the time and they might contact your ex. If you did not hide your IP address, you will be sorry when the cops coming looking for you.

WEBSITE REVENGE

This is a prank that is fun to pull on your friends, coworkers and ex's. This revenge can be light hearted or just a plain evil prank. You need to ask yourself how mean you want to go with this website revenge. If you plan on getting very nasty then let me say this.

You want to stay anonymous on this one, trust me. First things first, you need to hide your IP address. (see link just above this section title)

If you plan on just doing this to do a friendly prank you don't need to hide your IP. If you want to have real fun then I strongly urge you to buy that program and install it before you start the rest of this prank.

You will need an email address first. Go to Gmail, Yahoo or Hotmail and make an account for your victim. The next thing to do is set up an anonymous website. There are many free web hosting sites. And Geocities is a yahoo site, so you can just use the new Yahoo email to make it quickly.

Just use the templates that Yahoo provides and make it easy on yourself. If you're feeling nice just put up silly pictures and make their interests a bunch of childish things. Say their interests are unicorns, Beanie Babies and stuff like that.

Revenge Idea Upgrades

EVIL PRANK BONUS

If you want to get meaner then post unflattering pictures where the victim looks fat or stupid and send out an email to your friends saying look what I just found.

GETTING EVEN BONUS

Still want meaner? Post your victim's website with an obviously lesbian/bi-sexual overtone. Make it butchy and put links to a bunch of gay organizations. Combine this with the Gay Dating and have some real fun.

GETTING SERIOUS REVENGE BONUS

Take it a step further by exposing their sick fetishes. Photoshop in some leather hoods and some bondage and viola. Then make sure you post your new sites address all over the victim's town's Criagslist page.

To really get the most mileage out of website revenge, send some anonymous emails to the victim's friends and family. Just say, "I was just surfing this morning and came across this sight, have you seen it?" or "I can't believe this is Becky's web page, did you know she had this perverted side to her?"

That should start the rumor mill and the victim's friends and family will spread the address of the web page like a virus.

UNDERWEAR AND CONDOM REVENGE

If you have a house mate, ex or friend and can get access to their underwear you can have enormous amounts of fun. Let's start with the classics. Capture a

CLEAN pair you know they will be wearing soon and turn it inside out. Get some numbing sports cream and put it in the crotch area. You don't need much put it on lightly. You don't want it too greasy or slimy or the victim will find it. The victim won't notice it at first until they sweat a little. As soon as the moisture and oxygen hit, it will really start burning.

Revenge Idea Upgrades

EVIL PRANK BONUS

The other classic of course is to put itching powder in the underwear. Everyone has heard of this trick but it is still just an awful thing to do to someone. This particular itching powder is just plain vicious. Be careful not to get it on yourself.

GETTING EVEN BONUS

Messing with a condom is a pretty evil thing to do to somebody, but I am sure some jerks deserve it. Steal the victim's condom. You will also need a syringe to do this prank. You can load the syringe with sports balm or itching powder.

You must use a very small amount or the victim will know. Stick the needle into the condom package and inject a small amount of it in. If you also what to get the victims sex partner inject both sides of the condom package.

GETTING SERIOUS REVENGE BONUS

Underwear And Condom Revenge can also be done with hot sauce. Endorphin Rush hot sauce is some of the hottest hot sauce around. A note on this hot sauce, there are many hotter but if you go past 250,000 Scoville units it will probably burn the skin permanently, so you really don't even want to touch this stuff.

The way I discovered this stuff is through a group of my best friends. Basically, some of them got it on their hands and had sex later or used the bathroom and touched themselves. They described it as a horrible pain that would not stop burning. This stuff is just pure evil to put in condoms, underwear or toilet wipes.

GETTING AN EX FIRED

Getting An Ex Fired is pretty hardcore revenge. Sometimes, your ex is such a jerk they deserve full blown payback. We will examine some ways just to make them the butt of their office's jokes. Let's start with making them uncomfortable at work. For the first prank you will need to find a very unflattering picture of them. Then find a company that makes a life sized cardboard clone of them.

Have the clone delivered to their lobby for everyone to see when they come in. If the picture is funny enough their coworkers will never let them live it down.

Revenge Idea Upgrades

EVIL PRANK BONUS

If you want to step it up a level then do this prank. Before you do this, you will need to hide your IP address or you can easily get busted.

Get your victim's work phone number to the receptionist and the office's address. Now Google home based business info and visit those sites. You want to sign your victim up to ones that want your phone number and personal info. Only give them the victim's work phone number not your victims home number. You are looking for ones that say they will contact you after you enter your information.

What happens is these information collecting websites sell the info to telemarketers. Now if you do this on about 20 pages, the receptionist will get nonstop calls from telemarketers looking for your victim. This will go on for weeks possibly months. Just keep giving the victim's information out on these sites every few weeks. As a bonus do the same thing to their cell phone and all these calls will burn up their minutes and drive them crazy.

GETTING EVEN BONUS

If you have access to their work email you can also cause tons of problems doing the technique listed above. Hopefully their email is monitored and their boss will be tipped off that the victim is looking to start a home business, which leads right into the next revenge idea:

GETTING SERIOUS REVENGE BONUS

If you're really interested in Getting An Ex Fired you will want to find out who their main workplace competitor is. You will want to construct a fake rejection letter from the main competitor. You will want to send the letter to their work with no name listed so the receptionist will open it. The letter should say something like, "Dear (victim's name), After careful consideration we have to reject your application. We have to admit, your offer to bring over all your accounts from (victim's company) and information was very tempting but we were advised by or attorneys that this would be highly unethical. We are sorry and we want to wish you good luck in your job search." If you have access you can also leave this letter in the fax or copy machine for a fellow employee to "stumble" across.

Be sure if you do this to not leave fingerprints on the envelope or paper. You will also want to mail it from a mailbox that is not in your neighborhood.

IDEAS ON RUINING HER WEDDING

Does your victim deserve to have their wedding ruined? Want to try and break up a wedding because you the person they are marrying is all wrong for them? Do you think your best friend is marrying a tramp and you need to let them know? Perhaps you just want the victim to suffer because they are such a horrible person. I will give you a few ideas on how to get revenge by destroying the victim's wedding day.

The first idea is to try and strike before they get married. Convince the future spouse that the victim is unfaithful by spreading rumors using false emails and dating sites. Create a profile for your victim and try and start hitting on anyone that will talk to you. Give them your victim's name, phone of the future spouse and address.

Revenge Idea Upgrades

EVIL PRANK BONUS

Make the guests hate the marrying couple. Find out some of the people on the invite list and send them rude invitations. Suggest the gift they should bring and mention they should not come if they cannot afford to bring it.

Pretend to be the victim and go change their registry to nothing but outrageously expensive gifts.

GETTING EVEN BONUS

Find out all the details you can about the wedding. Wait until a week before and make some calls pretending to be the victim. Cancel their reception hall, band, photographer, cake, and so on. If you're lucky, the victim won't find out until it is too late. Even if the victim finds out and repairs some of the damage it will cause massive stress and confusion on their wedding day.

Another idea is to hire an advertising plane that can pull a banner to fly over the outdoor wedding. Have it say something like, "Don't marry that cheat!"

GETTING SERIOUS REVENGE BONUS

If you cannot stop the wedding you can wreck their honeymoon by canceling it. Cancel their flight and hotel. Anonymously report their car to the police and say they are acting like newlyweds to smuggle drugs across the border.

If none of this works and you can't wreck the wedding, you can send out rude thank you notes to the guest. Thank the guest for their cheap gifts.

Chapter 7
VERY GROSS PRANKS

Welcome to very gross prank and revenge ideas. Poop, pee and toilet attacks fall in the world of getting even. The site really would not be complete unless it contained this form of revenge.

Some artists use paint, others use metal and wood, but my true medium was poop. It adds a personal touch if you can use your own, but your dog will always be happy to give you a fresh supply.

This section walks a fine line between playing fun pranks on your friends and getting serious payback on your enemies. Some of these evil pranks are very crude but I am sure there are some people who appreciate this form of getting even.

If you are offended easily you will want to skip this chapter.

I hope you take pride in your work and maybe even get some action shots of your victims. If you get a funny or evil photograph of your victim please send it in (http://TheBestPrankBookEver.LupoLit.com). If you're truly ready to get your hands dirty with these prank ideas then please read on.

YOU HAVE BEEN WARNED!

THE POO CUP REVENGE PRANK

The Poo Cup Revenge Prank was used over and over for years by most of my college friends who were on my rugby team. I got more mileage from this one prank because it so funny and is definitely one of my favorites. The hardest part is pooping in the cup. If you are skilled enough to hold a large soda cup on your butt and poop into without getting it all over your hands, then kudos to you! Most people place a grocery bag in the toilet bowl and use the seat to pin it down. Poop in the bag then transfer the fresh stink pickle to the cup. If you want to avoid all this you can use dog poop out of the yard. I think that's kind of impersonal, but each to his own. Once you have a loaded cup you need to smuggle it into your victim's house. This works best if your victim is a slob. It is easy to hide an old soda cup when the house is filthy. Hide it either behind a couch or under a bed. In a few days the odor will attach itself to everything in the room. It takes a few days for the stink to really ripen. It will drive the victim crazy trying to figure out why his place stinks. The source of the funk will be very hard to pin down sometimes if the house is messy enough. Since this biological attack happens days later you will be long gone and hard to connect to the scene of the crime.

Prank Idea Upgrades

REVENGE IDEA BONUS

Find a good piece of trash while at your sloppy friend's house. Things like used pizza boxes, old soda cups or carry out food boxes. The best attack I ever pulled off was with a used nacho container in my friend's bedroom. I smuggled it out of the bathroom, pooped in it and smuggled it back to his room. Then, I hid it under his bed behind a bunch of dirty clothes. It took him days to figure it out and he was very pissed when he did. I was long gone and hard to connect to the scene of the crime. If you really want to leave a personal calling card behind so they know it was you, then leave an upper decker. Poop in the upper tank of the toilet instead of the bowl. If you're lucky this will float around for days before magically showing up in the bowl after your victim flushes.

GETTING EVEN BONUS

You will need to be alone long enough to pull off a multiple poo cup revenge prank. You will definitely want go to your victim's house when they are away. Bring multiple poop cups and a screw driver. Go to each room and unscrew the air conditioning registers and take them off. Then place the poop cup deep into the duct work. Put back the registers and, voilà, a perfect poo cup revenge gag! It will take the victim forever to locate the smell. Most of the time, they will never locate it and will have to live in the funk for weeks. When their house finally starts smelling normal, do this prank again.

GETTING SERIOUS REVENGE BONUS

Do the same poo cup revenge as above but before you sneak into your friend's house be sure to drive around the neighborhood and collect some road kill. Simply add the road kill to the poop cup and attack. Not only will the odor become absolutely unbearable, but you will also get the added bonus of fleas and mites that will infest the home.

DISAPPEARING TOILET PRANK

The Disappearing toilet revenge prank was a very fun one I used in college. My main target was the off campus rugby house. You will need help with this one so recruit a partner in crime. You will need to find a friend with some wrenches and knowledge of how to pull a toilet. Toilets are surprisingly easy to remove. Wait for you victim to leave for work or class and get into their house. Proceed to steal every toilet in house. When your victims rush home they will run to the bathroom, pull down their pants and then realize they are staring at a hole in the floor. The general panic runs through the house when they realize there is nowhere to poop except a hole in the floor. I actually pulled this off during a party one time. The party goers had been drinking too much, and ran into the bathroom only to find no crapper.

Prank Idea Upgrades

EVIL PRANK BONUS

Place the toilets around the kitchen table to replace the kitchen chairs. Then pull out the fine china and set the table. Feel free stage the kitchen with some other toiletries from the bathroom. You can replace the table mats with bathroom floor mats. You can also replace the paper towels with a roll of toilet paper.

GETTING EVEN BONUS

Everyone loves redneck yard art. Place the crappers in the front lawn, use them as planters and place flowers of them. Oh, you're a fan of modern art you say! Well by all means, arrange the toilets like modern art and make a design. Get your partner in crime and make a tower out of them on the front lawn. This will add the bonus of the victim's neighbors getting to see the art all day before the victim arrives home.

GETTING SERIOUS REVENGE BONUS

How do you think this lovely prank its highest level of revenge? Well, actually use the toilet in the kitchen or lawn of course! A good artist would leave their victim some intestinal sculpture for them to find after a nice hot day. After all that is what a crapper is for. Also set up a schedule to do this to the house about every two weeks until they remember to lock all their doors and windows.

POOP SMEAR REVENGE PRANK

This evil prank is very crude and not real imaginative but it is still very funny. Basically get some poop and find new, creative ways to get your victim to step in it or touch it.

The easiest attack is to lay poop land mines. Lay poop strategically in their walking path or in front of a door.

Prank Idea Upgrades

EVIL PRANK BONUS

Smear poop on a door knob or smear poop under a car door handle.

GETTING EVEN BONUS

Smear the poop on the victims car seat, if you are lucky they will be wearing nice clothes when the sit down. As an added bonus it will be difficult to get out of the upholstery.

Also it is fun to give someone the turd purse. Just hide a turd at the bottom of a purse and watch the fun when she reaches in and finds the surprise.

GETTING SERIOUS REVENGE BONUS

Smear the poop on your victim's favorite coffee mug handle or rim. You should also hit their toothbrush and shampoo; get it sham-poo, pun intended. Not only will they be disgusted about touching it or tasting it, but your crap will have been in their hair and lips also. If done right, the victim should experience The Poop Smear with all five senses.

SHAVING CREAM SURPRISE PRANK

This works great on sleepy people or drunks. I know this can work on hung-over men because my little sisters did this one to me after a hard night of college partying. Frankly this really works best on girls and women. For some odd reason which only women only know, females don't seem to look before they sit on a toilet seat. How many times have you heard women get mad about sitting on a toilet that was left up? Simply sneak into to someone's bathroom when they are sleeping and spray their toilet seat with shaving cream, whip cream, or spray cheese.

Prank Idea Upgrades

EVIL PRANK BONUS

If you have time, be sure to unscrew the light bulbs in their bathroom. This way the light won't function and the victim will not see the trap. When they get up in the middle of the night to pee they will find the surprise.

GETTING EVEN BONUS

Unscrew light bulb then put syrup, baking grease, itching powder or petroleum jelly on the seat. One other very evil option is to smear poison ivy all over the toilet seat. I really love itching powder, this stuff is just plain evil. All brands of itching powder are not are not equal. If done right it should leave a good butt rash.

GETTING SERIOUS REVENGE BONUS

Unscrew light bulb so they won't be able to see the seat well. Then put slow drying adhesive or slow drying oil based paint. The paint is the better choice because you victim will have to scrub their butt with paint thinner and a wire brush for hours to get it all off.

SIT AND SQUIRT PRANKS

I am embarrassed to admit the way I found this practical joke was when someone pulled it on me in 7th grade. This is now also a college classic that never gets old. All you have to do is set the trap. Go to your victim's toilet and lift the seat, get a ketchup or mustard packet and put a hole in one end. Carefully lay the toilet seat down so it pins the packet between the seat and the bowl. Make sure the hole in the packet points away from the toilet and towards the victim's legs. When the victim sits down the packet will squirt out all over the back of their legs.

Prank Idea Upgrades

EVIL PRANK BONUS

A fun way to do this prank without making a huge mess is to use a toilet seat squirter. This sprays water on the victims butt when they sit down. It will still scare the poop out of someone.

GETTING EVEN BONUS

The easiest way to upgrade the sit and squirt prank is to use multiple packets for a huge mess. Also try and find packets of hot sauce that will irritate the skin.

You can plant these at the office or a church. Anywhere you know people are wearing nice clothes which will be ruined forever.

GETTING SERIOUS REVENGE BONUS

This trick also works on other furniture in the house. Pull the cushion off a favorite chair or couch and place a large plastic sandwich bag filled with water or pee on the edge of the couch or chair. Point the opening of the bag away from the chair or couch and barely seal it. Be careful when you place the cushion back in place. When the victim sits they will be squirted with water or pee and the furniture will be soaked for days. The moldy smell from the furniture is an extra bonus that never really goes away.

Spray Back Pranks

This is another old school classic that still is easy to do. This one is fast and cheap to pull on someone, and you have probably had someone pull it on you. Here is how to set the trap. Lift the victim's toilet seat so you are just working with the bowl. Pull plastic wrap tightly across the bowl so they cannot see any wrinkles. The wrap will cling to the toilet bowl without the need for tape. Put the seat down to pin down the wrap. Trim or tuck away the excess plastic wrap hanging over the bowl so the victim cannot see it. When the victim starts to pee, it will spray all over the place.

Prank Idea Upgrades

EVIL PRANK BONUS

If you are lucky you will get a lady or a man who sits when they pee. A few things can happen here depending on the stream strength. Most likely they will feel the full spray back all over their butt and legs. There is a good chance it will get all over their clothes and shoes too.

GETTING EVEN BONUS

If you get real lucky they will drop a stink pickle without noticing the plastic wrap. If you pulled the plastic tight enough and if it is pinned down well, the intestinal sculpture will form a pile on top on the wrap and smear all over the victims butt.

GETTING SERIOUS REVENGE BONUS

You definitely want to pull this off when your victim is sick with explosive diarrhea. If you don't want to wait until they get sick naturally you can help them along. Just combine this revenge idea with Gut Check Pranks in the next section and laugh like crazy when the explosive diarrhea rebounds off the place wrap like a trampoline and sprays everywhere!

GUT CHECK PRANKS

This is again a classic with some new twists. Are you sick of your roommates, children or mooching friends raiding your refrigerator and eating your stuff? It is time to teach them a lesson the hard way. Use their favorite food and insert stimulant laxatives to ruin their world for the next 48 hours. You will want to use something with a strong taste like sugary baked goods or something salty.

Set the trap and wait. Enjoy watching the victims do a mad scamper to the bathroom when the pills kick in.

Prank Idea upgrades

EVIL PRANK BONUS

Liquid laxatives are surprisingly easy to hide in beer, punch or any flavored drink. If you use a liquid laxative the victim will usually consume much more of it. It also seems to last longer in the body. This prank is also very fun to combine with the Sit and Squirt Pranks.

GETTING EVEN BONUS

Hide all the toilet paper, wet wipes or anything else someone would use to wipe. Using extra strong glue you will glue the toilet seat to the bowl. Then glue the seat to the lid so it cannot be flipped open anymore. The victim will waste valuable time wrestling with the lid before they realize they can't get it open. By the time they give up it will be too late.

GETTING SERIOUS REVENGE BONUS

Combine hiding the toilet paper with the Disappearing Toilet or the Spray Back Pranks. By the time they figure out the toilet is gone it will be way too late. You cannot even imagine the type of mess they will make in their pants when the laxatives kick in.

TOILET SEAT PRANKS

There is just so much fun you can do with toilet seats. The standby of course is to just outright steal the seat. Have you ever tried to pinch a loaf when there is no seat?

It is not easy. I know women have perfected the hover technique for public restrooms, but men are too clumsy to do this. You can also place tacks on the seat and unscrew the light bulb.

Prank Idea Upgrades

EVIL PRANK BONUS

A great prank is to use a toilet seat firecracker called a Bang Toilet Seat Gag. It will make a loud pop when the victim sits down and literally scare the poop out of them.

Another funny prank is to use extra strong glue and glue the seat in an upright position for a lady victim. Women really hate this one. The easiest way to do this is to put the seat in an upright position and glue the hinges. It's damn near impossible to put down without completely breaking it.

GETTING EVEN BONUS

One of my favorite classics is to use shoe polish on a black toilet seat. This one is almost impossible to detect and a real pain to get off. If you just use the polish on the outside of the rim you might get lucky and they won't notice it when they get up and wipe. The black polish will give a nice black underwear track stain which looks like they didn't wipe at all.

GETTING SERIOUS REVENGE BONUS

Warning: this one can hurt someone. But it's just so damn funny. All you need to do is unscrew the hinges and carefully place the toilet seat back in place. When someone sits down it will side off the bowl. The victim will either fall off the toilet and hit the floor, or, if you are very lucky, they will fall into the toilet water they just used.

Flaming Bag of Poop Prank

This classic prank is probably the first one somebody ever learns about when they are a child. Even though it is old, it has to be included in this section on poop pranks. I have tried to add some twists to this classic to give it new life. In case you just moved to this country or have been living in a cave you don't know this one, let me explain it how it works. Load a paper bag full of poop and place it on your victim's front porch. Light it on fire, ring the door bell and run. Go hide in a bush so you can watch the victim try and stomp out the flaming bag of poop. If the victim is dumb enough they will stomp out the fire and get flaming poop on their shoes.

Prank Idea upgrades

REVENGE IDEA BONUS

You will want to use a grocery bag liner that is strategically ripped so the poop will explode out of the bag when stomped. Place the ripped plastic bag inside a paper one then load the bag with poop. Water it down the so the splatter radius is massively increased when stomped. Nothing splatters like diarrhea!

GETTING EVEN BONUS

Do the same as above but use your own pee to create a nice, soupy pee-diarrhea mix. Why not let your victim experience all your body's waste at one time?

GETTING SERIOUS REVENGE BONUS

While the victim is being splattered by the flaming bag of poop containing the secret pee diarrhea surprise, run to the back of the house and knock on the back door loudly.

YOU NEED TO RUN LIKE HELL AND GET OUT OF SIGHT!!! The victim will be so mad they will run through their house smearing the pee soaked crap into their carpet and tracking it all over their house.

PEE ATTACK PRANKS

The pee attack comes in so many forms. The basic idea is to use pee to smell up the victim's house. The old classic prank is to simply pee in your victim's house plants. Or, pee in a bunch of tiny cups and put them all over the floor. Unscrew the light bulb so the victim won't see it until too late.

Prank Idea upgrades

EVIL PRANK BONUS

If your victims have cats, then pee in your victim's kitty litter box numerous times. The litter won't be able to absorb this much pee and the stink will leak into the house. The victim might even think their cat has an enormous bladder.

GETTING EVEN BONUS

A sneaky way to do this is to hide pee in the house. Pull out the tray from under the refrigerator and pee in it. After a few days the smell will get into all their food. You can also pee in a humidifier and let it mist the smell all over the house.

GETTING SERIOUS REVENGE BONUS

Pee in a spray bottle and squirt it under locked doors or car windows that are cracked. If you want to get pee deep into a room with a locked door you will have to use this old classic technique for pee delivery. Find a very shallow cookie tray or plastic tray. Lay down some plastic wrap on the entire tray and pee in the tray. Very carefully load it into the freezer and freeze it. After you freeze it you can now remove it with the plastic sheet. Then peel the plastic sheet off and you should have a thin sheet of frozen pee. You can take this thin frozen pee ice and slide it under locked doors to melt into the carpet of your victim. You will have to use a long yard stick or wire to push the frozen pee deep into the room.

Chapter 8
HOLIDAY PRANKS

Nothing spices up the holidays like a good prank or practical joke. Holidays create a special opportunity to make mischief. I remember when we were kids we used to set aside nights around our school holidays just to go out and prank people. There are just so many great holidays that provide themselves as targets for good pranks.

Halloween pranks are always funny and pretty easy to do. Halloween night has been pranked so much that it is now associated with mischief. You will find some classic Halloween pranks here as well as some new twists.

Christmas is an overlooked and underrated holiday for pranks. This is a rookie mistake because the holiday is a great time to pull practical jokes. You will find some classic Christmas pranks here as well as some new ones.

The grandfather of all prank holidays is of course April Fool's Day. A true professional does not just strike on April Fool's Day but also attacks all month long. A true revenge artist will stretch this holiday out. Here you will also find some classic April Fool's Day pranks but some new ones too.

HALLOWEEN PRANKS

There are so many funny tricks you can pull on Halloween. I found sometimes it was more fun to screw with the group you're out trick or treating with than people's houses. Let's start there. Inevitably when you're going out trick or treating with a large group you will get split up. You want to get out in front of your victim so you go to the house before they do. Once you have a house lead on them you can start screwing with your victim.

One of the funniest pranks we did is tell people that the victim is diabetic. Say something like, "Hey, my sister is coming and she is dressed like a ghost. Please don't give her any candy because she is diabetic. She will deny it but please don't give her any."

This will piss your victim off when they get apples and oranges all night.

Prank Idea Upgrades

EVIL PRANK BONUS

There are lots of fun ways to screw with the candy you're handing out. There used to be these cheap little hard candies wrapped in bright foil that we always used to get as kids.

We realized these little candies looked just like bouillon cubes (the little salty squares you throw in soup). So we used to buy the candies to hand out and slip a few cubes in.

GETTING EVEN BONUS

Of course, you can step it up with your Halloween Pranks and hand out chocolate laxative candies. You will need to buy a similar looking chocolate candy and exchange the wrappers. Try to pick a common candy so that is does not get traced back to your house.

GETTING SERIOUS REVENGE BONUS

One of the funniest pranks is to leave a bowl out front full of a nasty liquid. You can use gelatin, vomit or even poop. Just fill the bottom of the bowl and then arrange the candies on top. When the victim reaches in they will get a surprise.

P.S. - This is not too smart to do in front of your own house. This prank is much funnier if you plant the bowl at a victim's house.

CHRISTMAS PRANKS

Holiday pranks can be so much fun. My group of friends and I would go spread our special form of holiday cheer. Christmas time can offer a special opportunity to do some unusual pranks.

There are the classic ideas like putting coal in your brother's stockings and drunken Christmas caroling. Another dirty trick is to pay a little kid to pee on Santa's lap, this is always funny.

I also have to mention screwing with people's lawn ornaments. Have fun and make a crime scene. Have the reindeer mauling Santa like a police beat down. Don't forget to use crime scene tape and draw some body outlines of elves.

Prank Idea Upgrades

EVIL PRANK BONUS

The best forgotten classic is to place an ad on Craigslist and use your victims address. Have the ad begging for used wrapping paper and boxes and broken toys for orphans. Don't forget to also ask for the used trees to be brought over and piled in the yard. You can also just go out the week after and collect a bunch of dead trees and plant them at your victim's house.

GETTING EVEN BONUS

If your victim has a real tree with a water dish, pee in it. If the victim has a dog he might start peeing on the tree too. If you really want to stink up the joint spray deer sent on the Christmas lights. The light will heat up enough and make the joint really reek.

GETTING SERIOUS REVENGE BONUS

Give inappropriate gifts to an office toy collection bucket. Wrap some adult sex toys and drop them in those buckets for ages 10 and down. Make sure it is one where they take wrapped gifts. Unfortunately you won't get to see the looks of horror on the parents faces, but you image in your head will be just as funny. If you're feeling bold do this to a nephew or niece so you can see the shock. Just slip an anonymous present under the tree. This will also work on uptight co-workers.

APRIL FOOL'S DAY PRANKS

There are just so many pranks you can do for April Fool's Day. You can use any prank in this book. So take your time and look around for just the right practical joke. Really anything can qualify for an April Fool's Day prank if it is preformed around that day. I will share some of the classic pranks with you commonly done on the grandfather of mischief holidays.

Prank Idea Upgrades

EVIL PRANK BONUS

Here is a short very list of pranks I have pulled off when I was a kid.

I called my mom from college and explained to her that I slept with a few girls and now my penis looked strange. I described it in detail including oozing, bleeding sores, green fungal growth and a fish smell. I finally busted out laughing and yelled April Fool's, after she finished searching through the medical book looking at nasty penis pictures for about 5 minutes.

GETTING EVEN BONUS

I kind of feel bad about this one but I called my brother and started a nasty rumor. I told him that one of my friends confessed to me that he was sleeping with my brother's wife.

He got very serious and said he was going to have a good talk with her until she admitted it. I felt too guilty and called back in a minute and yelled April Fool's before it got really out of hand.

GETTING SERIOUS REVENGE BONUS

I pranked my mom again and convinced her she had to come bail me out of jail for a prostitution ring I got caught running in college. I then also asked if she would bring enough money for my prostitutes so their parents wouldn't find out. I called her before she went to the bank and got money and yelled April Fool's.

April Fool's Email Prank

There are a ton of email pranks scattered throughout this book. Read the whole book and decide which ones you want to do. Some of the best email pranks are located in the Boyfriend and Girlfriend Revenge chapters.

Of course the most basic is to sign them up on a bunch of adult websites. Once you put their name down on a few it will be sold and they will get tons of spam for years.

Prank Idea Upgrades

EVIL PRANK BONUS

You can pretend you one of the victim's friends and get them to spill some dirt. Make an email account with your victim's friend's name on it. Try and pick a friend they don't see often and send an email telling the victim you have a new email address.

GETTING EVEN BONUS

Once you get your victim to admit their secrets you can now email them to their email list. Just wait for your victim to forward something like a joke to all their friends. There will usually be a huge address list attached. Then copy and paste her list into your address book and send out their juicy gossip.

GETTING SERIOUS REVENGE BONUS

You can also outright steal you victim's passwords using a key logger. Once you have their email password you can really embarrass them.

Chapter 9
PRANK CALLS

Some of my best memories as a child was staying up late during sleepovers and making prank calls. It was so fun we started taping our calls and invented crazier and crazier calls.

My friends would sit around and try and top each other. We would have contests to see who could keep the victim on the phone the longest while we invented sillier and more obnoxious calls. It sure was fun and prank calls provided hours of fantastic entertainment.

When we were little kids we thought this one was so funny. You would call a house around 20 times and ask for Dr. Harris. Then we would wait till night time and call the victim and say "This is Dr. Harris. Do you have any messages for me?" Hey, I know it was lame but to a ten year old that was funny!

Unfortunately sometime in the late '80s and early '90s our fun got ruined because of caller ID and call tracing. It got much more difficult to prank someone anonymously. Sure you could use *67 and block your phone number but the victim would refuse to pick up a blocked call. It was a sad time for us pranksters, but it is now time to rejoice. Prank calls are back and better than ever!

Thanks to prepaid phones, VOIP like Skype and caller Id spoofers the fun is back on. With a good caller ID spoofer you can change the Id your victims sees to anything you want. You could make a bunch of calls and insult people and harass people. Then use a caller id spoofer to make it appear like the victim called and left the nasty messages. It is a great way to get the victim in trouble and annoy them with angry callbacks.

With a caller ID spoofer and some imagination you can have some real fun. Think of all the places your victim will see on their caller ID.

Some funny prank calls using a caller ID spoofer could be to Planned Parenthood, Venereal Disease Treatment Clinic or Gender Reassignment Center.

Other funny prank calls you could do with a caller ID spoofer include holiday themes to screw with some little kids. The kid could get a call from an angry Santa, Dracula, Bogeyman, Wolf Man, Tooth Fairy or Easter Bunny.

Afterword

Just a word of advice:

Use some damn common sense before you try any of these things and always ask yourself if this joke will end with you being some huge prisoner's new girlfriend on the cell block.

Good Hunting,

Tarrin P. Lupo

www.ingramcontent.com/pod-product-compliance
Lightning Source LLC
Chambersburg PA
CBHW020509030426
42337CB00011B/297